The Gift of Tongues

EXAMINED

A DEFENSE OF THE GIFT OF TONGUES AND ITS ONGOING MANIFESTATIONS IN THE MIDST OF THE CHURCH

DR. RICKY ROBERTS

CREATION HOUSE PRESS

A STRANG COMPANY

THE GIFT OF TONGUES EXAMINED by Dr. Ricky Roberts
Published by Creation House Press
A Strang Company
600 Rinehart Road
Lake Mary, FL 32746
www.creationhouse.com

Unless otherwise noted, all biblical quotations come from the King James Version.

The translations of the fathers come from public domain or were done by Dr. Ricky Roberts.

Cover design by Kirk Douponce,
www.udgdesignworks.com
Interior design by David Bilby

Library of Congress Control Number: 2003105733
International Standard Book Number: 1-59185-234-X

05 06 07 08 — 8 7 6 5 4 3 2

Printed in the United States of America

To all those who still believe in the God of the miraculous.

Contents

Introduction

What is the biblical practice of speaking in tongues? In the Scriptures, speaking in tongues is the practice of the Holy Spirit giving the utterance of genuine languages to a person and directing them to speak them. The key point is that the person speaking does not know the language he or she is speaking.

For example, a member of a tribe in some remote part of South America who has never learned English may get saved and come under the direction of the Holy Spirit and begin to speak and pray in perfect English within the hearing distance of others. Therefore, the speaker—by his permission—is surrendering himself to the direction, supervision, influence and power of the Holy Spirit so the Spirit can use his tongue to speak audibly to a group of people.

In effect, a person becomes God's mouthpiece. The will and self-consciousness of the saint are still present—though yielded—and self-control is retained even in this state. (See 1 Corinthians 14:32.)

However, the biblical practice of speaking in tongues is not:

- ✞ Some psychological exercise that can be explained away as a mental illness such as schizophrenia.

- ✞ Some pathological exercise caused by organic neurological damage or the effect of drugs.

- ✞ Entering into an alternate state of consciousness in which one loses all self-control and surrenders to the will of some unknown power.

- ✞ Some type of ecstatic utterance in which the person speaking is void of all self-control or ability to stop it; nor is it some sort of learned behavior.

✝ The babbling of pagans that has been called
speaking in tongues by the critics. The babbling
of the pagans is either unconnected sound
spoken together that follows no pattern and no
type of grammar or the vain repetition of words.
Matthew 6:7 states: "But when ye pray, use not
vain repetitions, as the heathen do: for they
think that they shall be heard for their much
speaking."

Neither must speaking in tongues be considered a
litmus test for correct doctrine or a means to qualify all
truth. Nor can it be considered the evidence that a person
is saved or a mature Christian. Speaking in tongues does
not prove that a Christian who practices it is superior to all
others. The gift of tongues is not to be exalted above all
other gifts. (See 1 Corinthians 12–14.)

Furthermore, the gift of tongues must never be used as a
means to contrast those who "have" from those who "have
not." All Christians must be seen as those who have not. The
only One who can be seen as He who has is the Holy Spirit.

To conclude, all supernatural gifts that the Holy Spirit
endows a believer with should always make that person
more humble and thankful instead of more prideful. The
gifts are seen as perfect, though partial in function, and
without a fault; the willing vessel who is their recipient is
imperfect and fraught with many faults.

The controversy over the gift of tongues must be placed
at the door of ignorance and tradition. Tradition is truly
the central reason for this controversy. The tradition is one
of hating all supernatural manifestations, especially those
that come from God.

Many Christian denominations practice this tradition
today. They exalt themselves to the position of final judge
and jury of all supernatural manifestations. They condemn the supernatural manifestations of the Holy Spirit to
silence, ruling that they all come from Satan.

The problem with this is that if all supernatural manifestations are of Satan, then all that a saint cares for is an

illusion. In light of this verse, we see that this hatred truly grieves the Holy Spirit. Ephesians 4:30 reads, "And grieve not the Holy Spirit of God, whereby ye are sealed unto the day of redemption."

The fullness of the gospel is not preached in the denominations that hate the supernatural moves and manifestations of the Holy Spirit through His gifts. These churches have the gospel without power, without life.

Within these denominations is found a ritualistic form of worshiping God that is no better than any group who proclaims formalism above the Holy Spirit. Within these denominations is also found a representation of spiritual life, but it is void of any true substance.

In addition to this, these denominations are filled with religious and legalistic spirits. Unless God Himself destroys the influence of these spirits, they will succeed in keeping many believers from any Spirit-anointed ministry.

Such denominations also are filled with the moans and crying of the Holy Spirit as a result of His not having His place in their services. They have unwittingly followed the ancient heresy known as Alogianism. The Alogians denied the continuation of the gifts of the Holy Spirit in the ancient church.

The very hatred of all supernatural manifestations within these denominations is a stumbling block for them. It prevents them from fulfilling the gospel fully in accordance with what the apostle Paul taught in Romans 15:19, and in accordance with the teachings of the early church.[1]

The early church found success in its efforts to spread the gospel. The modern church as a whole is finding nothing but failure. Why? The early church knew that supernatural manifestations of the Holy Spirit would bring success against the forces of Satan. They saw this supernatural power prove the Word of God and Christianity to a pagan world. Remove these supernatural manifestations, and the church fails. Remove them, and the Word of God becomes lifeless.

We must not reverence the works of scholars who attack the gifts of the Holy Spirit (and especially the gift of tongues), neither should we rely on their works in order to find salvation and correct doctrine. There is only one book that we should give that kind of reverence. There is only one book we can rely on for judging and determining right from wrong, evil from good, and correct doctrine from incorrect doctrine. That book is the Bible.

Follow the Bible and not the wiles of tradition. Accept the Bible literally and not the fables of tradition.

I am faced with a bold work. How do I write about the gift of tongues with authority, while writing simply enough for all concerned?

The first edition of this book was a manual about the gift of tongues that was written to give as much indisputable evidence as possible of speaking in tongues still being for the church today. Many copies of it were sold, but many people asked for another simpler version.

I thought that perhaps I would write two separate versions of the same book. One would be a manual; the other would be a simple discussion. If I had done that, however, the simple version would have been less than fifty pages.

The only conclusion was to write a new version that would incorporate both visions. This was accomplished by adding at the end of each chapter an overview that gives in simple yet precise terms a summary of the preceding chapter. If you have any difficulty understanding a chapter, flip to the overview.

VERBUM IPSE DEUS

Text and Pronunciation Guidelines

NOTES ABOUT BIBLICAL TEXTS

All critical editions of the Greek New Testament were consulted when dealing with the New Testament and its doctrine of the gift of tongues and other gifts of the Holy Spirit. Both the critical and majority views were considered. The Greek New Testament will be known as the *Greek New Testament* or the *Greek text*.

The Hebrew text was consulted when dealing with the Old Testament. It is known as the *Masoretic Hebrew text*. Within this book it will be referred to by that name.

The Septuagint was also consulted when dealing with the Old Testament. The Septuagint is a translation of the uncorrupted Hebrew text and must be considered when studying the Old Testament. In this book it will be referred to as the *Greek Septuagint*.

PRONUNCIATION NOTES

The pronunciation of Greek used in this book is that of modern Greek instead of that derived from Erasmus. It is a known fact that modern Greek more resembles ancient Greek than the manner in which Erasmus pronounced Greek.

Byzantine scholars pronounced ancient and modern Greek in the same way. The pronunciations of ancient Greek even before the close of the first century are also found in modern Greek. In the fifteenth century the Greeks reportedly still pronounced the Greek language as Plato, Euripides and Aristophanes had.

In addition, papyri refute the Erasmian pronunciation. The vowels and diphthongs—coming from the Alexandrian period and written in Koine Greek—were not pronounced the same as the pronunciation of Erasmus. They were pronounced in the same manner as modern Greek.

The pronunciation of Hebrew used in this book is commonly used throughout colleges that still teach the language. It is considered almost universally to be the closest to the ancient Hebrew pronunciations.

To help you pronounce the various Greek and Hebrew words presented, transliterations have been provided in parentheses following each word.

Chapter One

The Term *Tongues* and Its Use: Part I

When dealing with the issue of the gift of tongues, the term *tongues* itself must be understood in the light of biblical history and the texts. However, this understanding cannot be limited to just biblical history and the texts, in particular the Greek Septuagint and the Masoretic Hebrew text.

The understanding that Christians must have of the gift of tongues is also connected to the Greek poets, Greek philosophers and the Apocrypha. Accordingly, God has set before the Christian a whole range of sources for preparing us to accept and experience the phenomenon of the gift of tongues. It appears God worked slowly to prepare mankind for this wonderful phenomenon of heaven.

While the focus of this chapter refers to sources outside of the Bible, the use of the term *tongues* in the Greek Septuagint and Isaiah 28:11 will also be discussed. Chapter two focuses on the thoughts and meanings of the term *tongues* in the New Testament apart from Acts and 1 Corinthians 12–14. Therefore, chapter two does not deal with the thoughts and meanings of the term *tongues* in the Old Testament. Other chapters will deal with the term *tongues* and how it is used in Acts and 1 Corinthians 12–14.

The connection between all of these sources and the gift of tongues is due to the Greek and Hebrew nouns that mean *tongues*. The most used noun is the Greek noun γλῶσσα (pronounced "glōsä"). To obtain a full understanding about the gift of tongues, one must understand a full meaning of the Greek and Hebrew nouns for the word.

GREEK POETS AND PHILOSOPHERS

The Greek poets and philosophers defined tongues as:

- ✝ The organ of taste
- ✝ The organ of speech
- ✝ The speaker himself or herself
- ✝ Speech
- ✝ Dialects of languages
- ✝ A language
- ✝ An expression seen as obscure or strange, which must have explanation

The Greek poets and philosophers understood that tongues could mean languages. To these men, however, these languages were both human and divine. They saw that the term *tongues* was also connected to the gods because the gods had their own languages.

For example, archeologists have found that in the Greek religion it was believed that the gods had their own divine language. Plato himself believed the gods spoke their own language and that each class had its own dialect. He believed those who are possessed by the gods do not speak their own language, but the language of the gods possessing them.[1]

APOCRYPHA

In the Apocrypha, especially the book titled Sirach, the term *tongues* is used to mean that the tongue is a scourge over all mankind. Also, in the Apocrypha, *tongues* mean "genuine languages." (See Judith 3:8 and Sirach 5:13.)

Fourth Maccabees 10:21, which was written between 63 B.C. and A.D. 38, reads: "But God will speedily pursue and seek for you. For you have cut off the singing tongue of angelic songs."

Notice! This ancient document proves that tongues cannot be limited to just human languages, human speech or even the physical organ of speech. Rather, it includes that this saint of God with his tongue was singing angelic songs in the language of heaven.

In 4 Maccabees 10:21, the Greek adjective θεῖος (thēōs) denotes that the songs found on this man's lips were angelic songs in the very language of heaven itself. What does this suggest?

☩ Before the dawn of Christianity, the Jews believed that angels spoke their own languages.

☩ Forms of speaking in tongues were present in a limited function in the Old Testament.

It must be noted that the gift of tongues had not yet been given during the Old Testament times. Yet, on special occasions, God would allow people of the Old Testament to sing and speak in tongues that were not their own. Why? It was a sign that this phenomenon would be present in the church—as well as to prove that the bondage of the law and strangling hold of paganism could not wholly hinder the moving of the Holy Spirit.

GREEK SEPTUAGINT

In the Greek Septuagint, tongues repeatedly mean the organ of speech, especially in Psalms, Job, Proverbs and the prophets. The theme here is the sins of the tongue or the sins spoken by the tongue. Within this translation, however, the idea of languages is still found with relation to the word *tongues*. The tongue is the organ of speech for speaking words that form different types or dialects of languages. Further, within Psalms, Job and Proverbs, there is present a strong characteristic of practical Jewish wisdom and that of ancient wisdom other than the Jews'.

Within Psalms, Job, Proverbs and Jeremiah the tongue is characterized as:

☩ What hatches evil (Ps. 51:4)

☩ A scourge (Job 5:21)

☩ A sword (Ps. 56:4)

☩ A bow and arrow (Jer. 9:3, 8)

✝ The sharp tongue of a horrible serpent (Ps. 139:3)

✝ A terrible weapon that can destroy people by what is said (Ps. 63:8; Jer. 18:8)

Proverbs 18:21 says that all the consequences of sinning with the tongue will come back on the one who has used it for evil. Accordingly, the reason for the exhortation not to commit sins of the tongue is that the result of such sins leads to other sins—deception, falsehood, arrogance and boasting.

In other parts of the Greek Septuagint, the tongues are seen as languages themselves. This is clearly seen in several scriptures: Genesis 10:5, 20, 31; Isaiah 28:11; 29:24; Daniel 3:2, 4; 7:14; Zechariah 3:9. From this again, God is preparing for the term *tongues* to be understood in the light of real languages being used in the gift of tongues and not gibberish.

ISAIAH 28:11 AS PERTAINING TO TONGUES

The rest of this chapter will deal with Isaiah 28:11 almost exclusively, since it is firm proof from the Old Testament that speaking in tongues was foretold for the church. Isaiah 28:11 reads, "For with stammering lips and another tongue will he speak to this people."

The tongue mentioned in this verse describes the experience of the gift of tongues as mentioned especially in Acts of the Apostles and 1 Corinthians. Paul himself uses this passage to indicate that the gift of tongues in a church meeting was a sign for unbelievers. (See 1 Corinthians 14:21–22.) Paul's view and understanding of the gift of tongues is founded on Isaiah 28:11–13.

If Isaiah 28:11 had not been present in the Old Testament, Paul and the rest of the apostles may have rejected this experience as not being genuine. One of the aims then of Isaiah 28:11 was to show that the gift of tongues was and is a divine gift from God and that this gift deals with genuine languages, not gibberish.

What is so glorious about Isaiah 28:11, in particular, is the fact that the gift of tongues is tied to the Old Testament. It cannot be shown to be some perversion of Christianity when it was foretold that the message of Christianity would also include the gift of tongues.

Apart from the gift of tongues being present with all other aspects of Christianity, our faith is seen as only partial, not full, not fully alive. So important was and is the gift of tongues that Isaiah was bewildered about what was said. It was a mystery in the midst of a mystery.

So important was it for the gift of tongues to be manifested in the early days of Christianity that God covered up what was meant in Isaiah 28:11–13. And if it was so important in the early days, it must be important today. So important was the gift of tongues that it was hidden from men, angels, Satan and all his evil forces.

Generally speaking, Isaiah 28:7–13 has been taken to denote a prophetic word against the kingdom of Judah. It prophesied that in just the same way that the kingdom of Israel fell by a Gentile kingdom, so would the kingdom of Judah fall, unless its people repented.

However, the context does not allow Isaiah 28:7–13 to be applied only to the past. Isaiah 28:11–13, in particular, deals with the future of Isaiah. Isaiah 28:11–13 does not deal with a prophetic warning against the Jews only in the kingdom of Judah. It is a prophetic word to all the house of Israel, including all the tribes. It is about a time when God Himself would speak differently to His people Israel through the gift of tongues.

The ancient church held no other interpretation for Isaiah 28:11–13 than it dealt with the coming of the gift of tongues. For example, Tertullian limits the interpretation of Isaiah 28:11–13 to that of the coming of the gift of tongues.[2]

In the ancient document, *The Constitutions of the Holy Apostles*, which was completely compiled before A.D. 325, Isaiah 28:11–13 is interpreted as a prophecy dealing with the coming of the gift of tongues. This passage is also seen as referring to God Himself speaking initially for His own people through the gift of tongues.[3]

It is very interesting that several Greek and Hebrew scholars have looked very carefully to Isaiah 28:10, seeing that there is a connection between it and Isaiah 28:13. They have concluded that Isaiah 28:10 is actually an interpretation of angelic tongues spoken by Isaiah. Even the interpretation itself was not truly understood by the people of Judah.

The phrase "with stammering" has been much misinterpreted. It has been connected to those speaking in tongues or to God. However, the very idea with stammering being connected to "lips" cannot grammatically be connected to those speaking in tongues or to God at all.

The idea expressed by the Greek and Hebrew texts is clearly connected to the Jewish people. It is a message that those on the Day of Pentecost would be seen by the onlookers in a horrible light.

At the first manifestation of the gift of tongues, the onlookers saw the gift of tongues as an object of contempt and mockery. Those who experienced the gift were laughed at, scorned, ridiculed and accused by the native Jews of being drunk on new wine. (See Acts 2:2–15.)

In fact, the very grammatical structure of both the Greek and Hebrew texts describes the onlookers of this mighty manifestation as having nothing but contempt for what was being done and spoken. This verse also indicates that God shows nothing but contempt for those who have contempt for speaking in tongues.

According to the Greek and Hebrew nouns, "stammering" is incorrect. The Greek noun φαυλισμός (phävlēsmōs) truly means "contempt, disparagement, slander and mocking" in the Greek Septuagint of Isaiah 28:11. The Hebrew expression בְּלַעֲגֵי (bəläägä) is commonly translated as "with stammering" in the Masoretic Hebrew text of Isaiah 28:11. It also means "contempt."

For this reason, this Hebrew expression is commonly understood to mean that God Himself will speak with stammerings of His lips. However, this Hebrew expression does not represent this at all. It is not God Himself who will by means of tongues do the stammering, but others. It is not God who will speak in contempt, but the Jewish people.

This thought has been hidden because of incorrect definitions and translations of this verse. Those lips of contempt were those of the Jewish people condemning the gift of tongues. Clearly, there is a contrast. The Jewish people were mocking and showing contempt for the gift of tongues, and God was showing contempt for them.

Think about it! God will defend His supernatural manifestations, whatever they are and whatever they will be.

Moreover, the Greek and Hebrew texts see the cause for the infusion of tongues on the Day of Pentecost and afterward as due largely to the contempt found on the lips of the Jews about Christ, His apostles and all aspects of Christianity. The contempt of the Jewish people covers the gift of tongues, Christ, His apostles and all other aspects of Christianity. In essence, the Jewish people found nothing good about Christianity.

Their contempt of the gift of tongues clearly is because on the Day of Pentecost, with the arrival of the Holy Spirit and the gift of tongues, God was setting His approval on Christianity and rejecting Judaism and paganism all at the same time.

Accordingly, it is others, even the Jewish people who will speak with stammering lips in contempt and mockery. If God were the One stammering, then it would be God Himself who was mocking and showing contempt over the death of Christ, the gospel, the apostles, the early church and in particular His own out-of-the-ordinary way of speaking to His people. God forbid!

The truth is, the texts show that it was the Jews' contempt—for God's speaking to them in this strange manner, as well as for Christ, the gospel, the apostles and the early church.

The singular sense of "lip" is used here for a plural

number so that one can well understand that the lips of the Jewish people are united in this contempt. The phrase "another tongue will he speak to this people" deals with God speaking differently to His people through the gift of tongues.

Further, the grammar of both the Greek and Hebrew texts indicates that because of the rejection of Christ by the Jews, the tongues were birthed as a sign of their temporary rejection by God and His acceptance of the Gentiles and believing Jews in their place. (See Matthew 10:18; 11:11–27; 17:12; 21:3–46; John 1:11; 5:16–18; Romans 1:16; 9:30–10:21; Acts 15; Galatians 2:3; Colossians 2:14–17; Hosea 5:14–6:2; Isaiah 8:14; 28:16; Deuteronomy 32:21.)

Consequently, the practice of speaking in tongues was and is, in all its perspectives, a negative sign for the unbelieving Jew. It was also and is a positive sign for the believing Jews and Gentiles and a positive sign for the unbelieving Gentiles. In both the past and present the practice of speaking in tongues indicates the temporary rejection of the unbelieving Jews by God, the hope of salvation for the unbelieving Gentiles, and the acceptance of the believing Gentiles with the believing Jews in the place of the unbelieving Jews.

On the Day of Pentecost, the manifestation of the gift of tongues was a message of warning to all the house of Israel of what would happen to them if they, as a whole, rejected Christ as the Messiah.

What would be the results of such a rejection? The Jews would stumble, fall and collapse before the Messiah and finally be destroyed as a nation. (See Romans 9:32–33; Luke 21:20–24.) Isaiah 28:13 confirms that the Jews would be broken as a nation as a result of their rejection of Jesus Christ as Messiah. (See Romans 11:7–29; Matthew 21:42–44; Luke 20:18.)

In 1 Corinthians 14:21–22, Paul warns unbelievers of God's attitude toward them by using the Greek noun σημεῖον (sēmeōn). This indication, token or sign by which something is known is viewed by most modern commentaries as a judgment by God on unbelievers (Jews or Gentiles). However, the gift of tongues as a sign, according to Paul, is a warning. It is a warning and a call to unbelievers for conviction, not condemnation.

According to Greek grammar, which uses the *dative of advantage*, the gift of tongues is seen by Paul as being for the benefit of unbelievers, not for believers. This benefit must be considered as positively calling them to salvation.

In contrast, the gift of prophecy is for the benefit of believers, not unbelievers. If the gift of prophecy is a positive benefit for believers, then the gift of tongues must also be a positive benefit for unbelievers. The scriptures about the purpose of each gift must be true in both cases.

One cannot demand that the gift of tongues is a negative benefit for unbelievers while the gift of prophecy is a positive benefit for believers. One cannot have it both ways here. According to the same Greek construction used four times, both the gift of tongues and the gift of prophecy have a positive benefit, but on different groups of people. This positive benefit is still seen, even if unbelievers accuse people of being drunk or mad. (See Acts 2:1–15; 1 Corinthians 14:23.)

Paul does not deal with the negative sign of speaking in tongues in 1 Corinthians 14:21–22, although it is present in Isaiah 28:11–13. That can be inferred. He does not deal with the positive sign of tongues for believers as clearly seen in Isaiah 28:11–13.

He simply does not bring these two other perspectives into his dialogue in 1 Corinthians 14. For Paul, the gift of tongues is seen only as denoting a positive sign for unbelievers—unsaved Jews and Gentiles—in the sense of being used for conviction, nothing more. (See 1 Corinthians 14:21–22.) Paul does not deny the other significant aspects of the gift of tongues. He simply chooses not to address them.

The gift of tongues was and is a sign that the message

of the gospel was and is ever intended for every creature. It also was and is the very office of the Holy Spirit to restore the unity of language and the unity of humanity in the Christian community.

Both the Greek and Hebrew texts in Isaiah 28:11 speak in prophecy of a new type of language that will come forth in the times of the apostles.

The adjective "other" in the Greek text comes from the Greek adjective ἕτερος (ĕtĕrōs), which means "another of a different kind." The adjective cannot be used to prove that the language only deals with human languages. The purpose here is that the languages, whatever they may be, will not be spoken by the receiver's own power but by the unction or utterance of the Holy Spirit.

This is the "different kind" meant here and also in Acts 2:4. The difference then—stressed here—is not of origin, nature or rank but is dependent on the situation in which it is used, its purpose, and especially how it is used.

Notice that the Greek adjective ἕτερος (ĕtĕrōs) is used to describe those who mocked this supernatural utterance of the Holy Spirit. (See Acts 2:13.) Those who mocked this were humans, not angels. The difference here was not a difference of race, nature or rank. It was one that ranged from doubting the event to mocking and blaspheming it. So, the real difference is how each group viewed this manifestation of the Holy Spirit.

The Hebrew adjective אַחֵר (äkhĕr) is well understood as conveying the same meaning as the Greek adjective. Both the Greek adjective and Hebrew adjective can well exhibit a "strange language" rather than "another" language. This leads to the conclusion that "speaking in tongues" is not a natural occurrence but a strange occurrence and one that is done by utterance of the Holy Spirit.

OVERVIEW OF CHAPTER ONE

1. The Greek poets and philosophers defined tongues as:

✝ The organ of taste
✝ The organ of speech
✝ The speaker—himself or herself
✝ Speech
✝ Dialects of languages
✝ A language
✝ An expression seen as obscure or strange, which must have an explanation connected to it

2. The Apocrypha defined tongues as:
✝ The scourge of all mankind
✝ Genuine languages
✝ Angelic languages

3. The Greek Septuagint defined tongues as:
✝ The organ of speech
✝ Languages—whether human, angelic or divine. (See Genesis 10:5, 20, 31; Isaiah 29:24; 28:11; Daniel 3:2, 4; 7:14; Zechariah 3:9.)

4. Within Psalms, Job, Proverbs and Jeremiah in the Greek Septuagint, the tongue is characterized as:
✝ What hatches evil. (See Psalm 51:4.)

✝ A scourge. (See Job 5:21.)

✝ A sword. (See Psalm 56:4.)

✝ A bow and arrow. (See Jeremiah 9:3, 8.)

✝ The sharp tongue of a horrible serpent. (See Psalm 139:3.)

✝ A terrible weapon that can destroy people by what is said. (See Psalm 63:8; Jeremiah 18:8.)

5. Isaiah 28:11–13 describes the gift of tongues mentioned in Acts of the Apostles and 1 Corinthians. It has a variety of applications:
✝ Isaiah 28:11–13 is a prophecy dealing exclusively with the gift of tongues and its arrival on the Day of Pentecost.

✝ It is firm proof that the gift of tongues is not a perversion of Christianity.

✞ It indicates that the gift of tongues is a divine gift, not a gift from Satan.

✞ Paul studied Isaiah 28:11–13 and based much of his view of the gift of tongues on it.

✞ Isaiah 28:11–13 shows that the gift of tongues was a mystery in the midst of a mystery that Isaiah himself did not understand.

✞ Isaiah 28:11–13 historically has been interpreted as dealing with the gift of tongues by the early church.

✞ Greek and Hebrew scholars believe that Isaiah 28:10 is actually an interpretation of angelic tongues spoken by Isaiah.

✞ The phrase "with stammering" is not connected with those speaking in tongues, nor with God, but with the Jewish people.

✞ The stammering deals with contempt and mockery wrought by the Jewish people.

✞ The contempt by the Jewish people was due largely to God setting His approval on Christianity.

✞ The gift of tongues was birthed as a sign of the temporary rejection of the Jewish people by God.

✞ The gift of tongues is a negative sign for the Jewish people.

✞ The gift of tongues is a positive sign for the believers.

✞ The gift of tongues is a positive sign for the unbelieving Gentiles.

✞ The gift of tongues indicates the hope of salvation for the unbelieving Gentiles.

✞ The gift of tongues indicates the acceptance of the believing Gentiles and Jews in the place of the unbelieving Jews.

Chapter Two

The Term *Tongues* and Its Use: Part II

In Chapter One the reader follows the path set forth by God, even before the dawn of the New Testament, for the revelation of the gift of tongues. The revelation of the gift of tongues was slowly but surely painted as a great masterpiece before the world and before the Jewish people.

This revelation was hinted at, spoken of and revealed only in the mist of legalism, the bondage of the law and the strangling of the world by paganism. Indeed, the revelation of the gift of tongues was seen to be a high gift and a high advancement of religion and of the cause of God. This coming forth could not be in the midst of Judaism or paganism. It required a refreshing, a holy vehicle to achieve success.

That holy vehicle could only be a new and full experience of God without any bondage from the law or paganism. That holy vehicle could only be Christianity birthed by Christ.

Following the landmarks laid down by God through the Old Testament, Greek poets, Greek philosophers and the Apocrypha, the background of this subject is understood. In addition, the thought and meaning wrought by Christ and the apostles are seen to be a fulfillment of what has already been given.

In other words, the revelation previously given about the gift of tongues is brought to its rightful and complete resting place in the New Testament. It is first founded by Mark 16:17 and completely established in structure in Acts 2 and 1 Corinthians 12–14. Therefore, it is now brought to fruition, and God reveals completely what was hidden as a mystery within a mist.

Now the reader turns his attention to the New Testament and sees that the use of the Greek noun γλῶσσα (glōsä) in the New Testament—outside of the Book of Acts and 1 Corinthians 12–14—is most restrained and narrow in thought and meaning. The dominant use of this Greek noun (outside of Acts and 1 Cor. 12–14) is in describing the organ of speech.

It is found throughout the New Testament. (See 1 John 3:18; James 1:26; 3:5–6; 1 Peter 3:10; Mark 7:33–35; Luke 1:64; 16:24; Romans 3:13; 16:10.) It is even defined as such in Acts 2:26.

However, in the Book of Revelation, this Greek noun is constantly found to denote "languages," in particular "human languages." (See Revelation 5:9; 7:9; 10:11; 11:9; 13:7; 14:6; 17:16.)

A STUDY OF MARK 16:17

The focus of this chapter is to determine just what is meant by tongues in Mark 16:17. This verse lays the New Testament foundation for what is mentioned in Acts and 1 Corinthians 12–14. It serves as a direct link between the Old Testament and the other books of the New Testament with regard to the phenomenon of speaking in tongues.

Therefore, apart from understanding Mark 16:17, like that of Isaiah 28:11–13, one cannot receive a complete perspective of the gift of tongues. Not understanding Mark 16:17 is the cause of much confusion over this gift.

Accordingly, in Mark 16:17, the use of the Greek noun γλῶσσα (glōsä) is connected historically and grammatically to Acts 2 and 1 Corinthians12–14 in the practice of speaking in tongues.

In Mark 16:17, the Greek verb λαλέω (läleō) is found in

the third person plural and is connected to the *aorist tense* participle πιστεύσασιν (pēstĕfsäsēn), used in the Greek text.

The type of aorist tense is the *progressive aorist.* The progressive aorist stresses the results of believing in Christ and having adopted the Christian faith. Consequently, the act of believing is not stressed here, but the results of being in that glorious state of redemption are.

The results of believing and accepting Christ as Savior are named afterward. In other words, it is the after-effect of salvation on a person's life that is being pointed to in Mark 16:17. Notice that to Christ and the apostles the after-effect of salvation should include the miraculous. It is shown here that a Christian life without the miraculous, though a Christian life indeed, is incomplete.

The historical view of Mark 16:17–18 leads in two directions that dominated the early church. The first position represented in the early church is that the signs here mentioned are for all believers and eventually all these signs will be manifested by them. The second position represented in the early church is that all believers do not manifest these signs. The later view is the one supported by Greek grammar.

The promise mentioned in Mark 16:17 is valid not only for the apostles, but also for Christians in general. The use of the aorist tense cannot be grammatically and historically limited to the apostles only. If the aorist tense can be limited to only the apostles, then only they and they alone were ever saved and redeemed by the blood of the lamb.

Moreover, it is not necessary for all these signs to be functioning through all the believers. Rather, some of these signs may never manifest themselves through believers. Other signs may manifest themselves through a certain believer only for a time and from that point on be dormant but never active again. These signs will follow and accompany all of the church, but not all saints will experience all the phenomena.

This can be seen through two arguments:

✞ The apostles themselves did not exercise all these signs. In the Book of Acts, all these signs are seen, except drinking poison. Therefore, there must be some limit or conditional element to these signs that cannot be seen through the English but are clearly seen in Greek grammar.

✞ Within Mark 16:17–18, the *subjunctive mood* is used in the Greek text.

This last argument is very striking. The subjunctive mood demands that drinking poison and taking up serpents were and are seen only as probable signs of believing. They may occur or may not occur. They may occur in one person's life and not in another person's.

In other words, they only can occur when they are enacted by another's will—whether Satan's, his satanic forces' or another human's—not by the receiver's own will. The sign of drinking poison without being harmed is not the result of receiving poison from one's own self, but from another. It is another who gives the poison to the believer so he will drink it, and the believer then unknowingly drinks the poison.

The same is true of taking up serpents. The serpents are unwittingly placed in the path of the believer by Satan and used by Satan to bite the believer. There is no intention here of the believer willingly picking up serpents. It is not in the ability of the believer to initiate this sign. Rather, it is someone else who initiates it.

In this case, the use of the subjunctive mood in verse 18 brings forth from Mark 16:17–18 the thought of uncertainty and plausibility and concentrates on the ability to choose and to reject. It indicates that not all of these signs will be closely following all believers, but only that they may or may not. The will, whether of the believer or someone else, is placed within the equation spoken here by Christ.

Subsequently, the use of the subjunctive mood by Christ

shows that He foresaw two divisions within Christianity:

☩ One division would accept the reality of these signs and anticipate their manifestations in modern times, especially seeking the signs of speaking in tongues, casting out demons and praying for the sick to recover.

☩ The other division would not accept the reality of these signs and would not anticipate their manifestations in modern times.

Hence, the subjunctive mood indicates that some would not speak in tongues because they will not accept the gift of tongues as still being in operation. Others will truly speak in tongues, for they have seen and recognized that the gift of tongues still continues, and they will desire all that God has for them.

Some will reject any believer casting out demons in the name of Jesus, while others will experience that sign. Some will reject praying for the sick, while others will accept this sign and find results. The person who is prayed for may recover or may not recover, as is seen in Greek grammar and Greek thought. It is not between the one praying and the one being prayed for but between God and the one who receives prayer.

According to the Greek grammar used in Mark 16:17, the tongues cannot be limited just to human languages. They must include all types of languages. The Greek noun γλῶσσα (glōsä) also informs readers that Christ did not mean that the gift of tongues would be equipped with pronunciations and sounds of gibberish or jargon, but that it would be intelligible languages.

The gift of tongues will only include genuine languages that make sense and can be understood by someone. The focus is never on gibberish and babbling. It is always on genuine languages that someone, somewhere can understand.

The statement about tongues in Mark 16:17—it must be fully stated from Greek thought and context—applies generally to Christians in all times until the time of the "perfect state." (See 1 Corinthians 13:8–13.)

There is a hint in Mark 13:11 that the gift of tongues would be given at the event of Pentecost.

The signs, mentioned by Christ after His resurrection, are found in three divisions:

1. The first division deals with the overthrow and destruction of evil in the form of casting out demons while contrasting the new form in the life of believers manifested by speaking in tongues.

2. The second division deals with the protection from physical creatures while contrasting the protection from all physical poisons through the overpowering life of Christians.

3. The third division deals with the removal of physical suffering from others while contrasting the return of the perfect feeling of health to those who believe.

The constant thought, by some, that the term *serpents* is actually a reference to demons is without merit. The Greek noun ὄφις (ōfēs) is understood by almost all authorities of Greek to be real serpents. If demons had been meant by the term serpents in Mark 16, the term "serpents" would have been used in the first division in Mark 16:17–18 rather than the second.

The second division deals with physical things, not spiritual things. Further, the Greek noun ὄφις (ōfēs) in the Greek Septuagint is almost exclusively used to denote real serpents. The Greek noun ὄφις (ōfēs) is commonly used to denote the "serpent" as a member of the species of serpents, while other Greek nouns deal with individual types.

Seldom, as in Luke 10:19, does this Greek noun denote demons. A difference between this Greek noun and other Greek nouns does not prove that demons are meant in Mark 16:17–18 either.

Furthermore, the expression, "If they drink anything poisonous," cannot mean anything but drinking poison in liquid form.

ARGUMENTS FOR THE GENUINENESS OF MARK 16:9–20

1. There are more than 5,000 Greek manuscripts. Of those that have the Gospels, only a few do not contain Mark 16:9–20. Consequently, manuscript evidence overwhelmingly supports these verses.

2. The Syriac version of the New Testament (translated in A.D. 150) contains these verses.

3. The Latin versions of the New Testament (which were copied from Jerome's Vulgate, A.D. 382) contain these verses. The Old Latin (which was translated in the second century) also contains these verses.

4. The Gothic version (translated A.D. 350), the Egyptian version (translated in the fourth century) and the Thebaic version (translated in the third century) all contain these verses.

5. The Armenian version (translated in the fifth century) and Georgian version (translated in the sixth century) all contain these verses.

6. More than 100 leaders of the early church include these verses in their writings. This evidence extends from the second century to the third century and beyond. Therefore, these leaders come to one's aid and indicate that these verses are truly part of the original text.

7. The internal evidence of the Greek New Testament supports the genuineness of Mark 16:9–20 very well. Compare Mark 16:9–20 with that of Mark 1:9–20. The style and manner found in each passage is the same and very clearly that of Mark. Further, within Mark 16:9–20, one finds every principal characteristic of Mark's style and manner. Phraseology also supports that Mark 16:9–20 was written by Mark.

8. The lectionary practice of the ancient church clearly furnishes a strong clue for unraveling why these twelve verses are absent from some manuscripts. Very early in the church it was customary to collect certain passages of the Scriptures into separate books so that they could be read in the

churches. Herein lies the problem. Some lections have segments that are collections not of Scripture but of sayings or beliefs in the church. It is for this reason that some scholars have denounced Mark 16:9–20 as forgery. They have concluded that Mark 16:9–20 is a forgery or a collection of beliefs in the early church collected from apostolic authority and tradition, apart from being derived from Scripture. But it cannot be proved that Mark 16:9–20 is fabricated just because it is part of the lections. Rather, it is seen that Mark 16:9–20 is genuine, since it is not found in any segment that is recognized as fictitious.

9. Victor of Antioch gives arguments to support the genuineness of Mark 16:9–20:

☦ Some copyists deliberately omitted these verses for one reason or another.

☦ The reason for their omission cannot be determined for lack of manuscript evidence, but it must be due to the judgment of individuals. Evidently, the copyists thought that the verses were inconsistent with the other verses found in the other Gospels. This is not the case.

☦ Victor became convinced of these verses' authenticity by the constant witness of so many voices.

☦ The Palestinian copy contained these verses and is seen as representing the original text of Mark's Gospel.

OVERVIEW OF CHAPTER TWO

1. Mark 16:17 lays the New Testament foundation on the issue of tongues.

2. It serves as a direct link between the Old Testament and the other books of the New Testament.

3. Without correctly understanding Mark 16:17, it is impossible to understand the gift of tongues

and the phenomenon of speaking in tongues.

4. Grammatically, Mark 16:17 is tied together with Acts 2 and 1 Corinthians 12–14. The same phenomenon mentioned in Mark 16:17, as dealing with tongues, is also found in Acts 2 and 1 Corinthians 12–14.

5. The Greek *aorist tense deals* with the results of being redeemed.

6. Historically, the church interpreted Mark 16:17 two ways:
   ☩ The signs are for all believers, and all believers will manifest the signs.
   ☩ The signs are for all believers, but not all believers will manifest the signs.

7. The promise mentioned in Mark 16:17 is not only for the apostles, but also for all believers.

8. By the use of the *aorist tense*, the promise cannot be limited to the apostles. It is for all believers.

9. By the use of the *aorist tense*, the signs cannot be seen as functioning in all saints at all times.

10. The signs will follow and accompany all of the church, but not all saints will experience these phenomena.

11. The apostles did not exercise all of the signs mentioned in Mark 16:17.

12. The *subjunctive mood* shows that, due to free will, not all of the signs will follow all believers.

13. The *subjunctive mood* indicates two divisions within the church:
    ☩ Those who will accept the reality of these signs.
    ☩ Those who will never accept the reality of these signs.

14. The tongues mentioned in Mark 16:17 cannot be limited to human languages but must include all types of languages.

15. The tongues mentioned in Mark 16:17 cannot be gibberish or jargon, but they must be intelligible languages.

16. The foundation of the promise mentioned in Mark 16:17, especially about speaking in tongues, is seen in Mark 13:11.

17. The signs are found to be in three divisions:
   ✝ The overthrow and destruction of evil, while contrasting the new experience in the life of believers.
   ✝ The protection from physical creatures, while contrasting the protection from all physical poisons.
   ✝ The removal of physical suffering from others, while contrasting the return of the perfect feeling of health.

18. The serpents mentioned in Mark 16:17 are real serpents, not demons. If demons had been meant, the term "serpents" would have been put in the first division rather than the second division.

19. The genuineness of Mark 16:9–20 is highly defended:
   ✝ There are more than 5,000 Greek manuscripts.
   ✝ The Syriac version of the New Testament contains these verses.
   ✝ The Latin versions of the New Testament contain these verses.
   ✝ The Gothic version, the Egyptian version and the Thebaic version all contain these verses.
   ✝ The Armenian version and Georgian version all contain these verses.

☦ More than 100 leaders of the early church include these verses in their writings.

☦ The internal evidence of the Greek New Testament supports the genuineness of Mark 16:9–20 very well.

Chapter Three

The Event of Acts 2:2–4

The event of Pentecost, as recorded in Acts 2, belongs to the same situation and context as mentioned by Paul in 1 Corinthians 12–14. This "speaking in other tongues" bears essentially, only with some differences, the same characteristics as the phenomenon depicted by Paul. It is the functioning of the same gift and comes from the same source. The same source is the Holy Spirit. This phenomenon is an endowment of the Holy Spirit. (See Acts 2:4.)

The mystery surrounding Isaiah 28:11–13 and the gift of tongues in New Testament times was ripped asunder by Mark 16:17 and manifested and defined in the event of Acts 2. The second chapter of Acts is the revelation of the gift of tongues, while Mark 16:17 uncovers what was meant by Isaiah 28:11–13. Further, Acts 2:2–4 demonstrates the reality of the promise mentioned in Mark 16:17, while Mark 16:17 demonstrates the promise of Acts 2:2–4.

The event mentioned in Acts 2:2–4 is the first manifestation of the gift of tongues for the church. While Christ had been baptized into the fire of all the nine gifts at His water baptism, the church's experience with the gifts of the Holy Spirit began at Pentecost. (See Matthew 3:1–17.)

The event of Acts 2:2–4 is of the highest importance for understanding the success of the early church. Within this event, the early church was transformed from a hopeless and useless vehicle to a vehicle filled with power for service and filled with great promise wrought by the power of the Holy Spirit. From this event, it is well learned that the success of the early church depended more than anything else on the empowering of the Holy Spirit with His gifts and fruits.

The modern church is failing because it does not want to go back and learn again what the people had already learned on the Day of Pentecost. The church must go back, seize what it once had, and use it to reap the success that it once had. The success of the early church was not due to large congregations, buildings and other material-istic achievements. Its success was having the ability to reap a great abundance of converts, healings, miracles, signs, wonders and other manifestations of the Holy Spirit.

Therefore, the quest of the modern church to recapture its empowerment must always begin at the center stage of the empowering by the Holy Spirit found in the early church, which is seen in Acts 2:2–4. It cannot begin any-where else.

To understand the empowerment of the early church, Acts 2:2–4 must be studied in the light of how the early church interpreted this passage of Scripture. Because so much importance is found in Acts 2:2–4 then, it will be the focus of this chapter.

ACTS 2:2

Acts 2:2, translated literally from the Greek text, states: "And suddenly there came instantaneously out of heaven a noise as of a rushing violent (and mighty) wind, and it filled instantaneously most of the house where they were sitting."

As Greek scholars study Acts 2:2, they begin by under-standing the tense of the Greek verb γίνομαι (yēnōmě). This Greek verb is found to be in the type of aorist tense known as a *momentary aorist*. The momentary aorist is an indication that something new is coming. The something new was a new state of Christian experience.

Understand that apart from this new state of Christian experience, there cannot be any empowerment of the saints. The saints are seen as powerless to the demonic and the fiery darts of the demonic.

The momentary aorist being used by Luke alone denotes that the new state of Christian experience was not coming in minutes, years or seconds. In reality, the power of the momentary aorist indicates that this new state of experience, this new light, this new revelation, this new level of Christian life and Christian experience were instantaneous in their coming. It was instantaneous, spontaneous and sudden.

The Greek adverb ἄφνω (äfnō) expresses that this immediate, instantaneous, and spontaneous incident was a shock and a surprise to those who were assembled on the Day of Pentecost. The apostles and others there were not looking for such an event, so extraordinary and impressive. There is no indication in the text that those present truly understood the magnitude of fulfillment of the promise. (See Acts 1:4–11; Luke 24:49; Matthew 3:11; 18:18; John 1:31–33; 7:39; 14:12–17.)

The phenomenon mentioned in Acts 2:2 originated not from the earth but from heaven itself. This is clear from the phrase "from the heaven." In Greek, this expression is known as the *ablative of source.* What does it mean, though? The ablative of source shows that the source of this new phenomenon is not earthly but heavenly.

Further, this expression must be seen as a sign that Christianity alone received its origin from heaven. Indeed, the very noise that came instantaneously from heaven was God setting His sign of approval on Christianity, showing that Christianity alone had received its origin from heaven.

In Acts 2:2, the word *sound* comes from the Greek noun ἦχος (ēkhos). According to this Greek noun, this sound, or noise, may be described in several ways:

✝ Heavenly

✝ Frightening

✝ Amazing

✝ Bewildering

✝ It caused those who heard it to turn their attention to it.

✝ It was the very noise of heaven in all its glory and with all its faculties.

✝ It was heard by all of God's angels, all of the satanic forces and all those who were in Jerusalem.

✝ It transcended the spiritual realm and entered the physical realm.

✝ It was such a noise that all who had an ear could hear it.

✝ It was a noise that revealed a new experience to the Christian.

✝ It was a noise that indicated a new walk in the Spirit to the Christian.

✝ It was such an awesome noise that it indicated the coming of the Holy Spirit in all His fullness in this life.

✝ It was the chosen vehicle by the Holy Spirit for Him to be manifested in all His glory and fullness to man's sense of hearing.

✝ It was an external manifestation and sign that attended the outpouring of the Holy Spirit.

✝ Nothing like this had ever occurred. It is as if this "noise" of heaven had been held back until this special time.

✝ It was the noise of the herald proclaiming the arrival of the Holy Spirit in all His splendor and all His power and fullness.

✝ It was the indication that the limitation of the Holy Spirit would be brought to an end, and the beginning of the fullness of the Holy Spirit would begin.

✝ Also, it was the very demonstration that God

Himself was fulfilling His promise of the Comforter, coming and outpouring Himself through the baptism. (See Acts 1:4–11; 11:15; Luke 24:49; Matthew 3:11; 18:18; John 1:31–33; 7:39; 14:12–17.)

✝ What was heard was the very breathing or blowing of the Holy Spirit on those present.

✝ It accompanied the descent of the Holy Spirit and echoed throughout all of creation.

✝ So awesome was this noise that it shook the very foundations of hell.

✝ It was a demonstration again that Satan had failed.

✝ It was truly audible when it instantaneously entered the house where the people were sitting.

✝ The noise was so loud that it was heard throughout Jerusalem.

✝ This noise was of such a nature that it could well be heard in both realms: spiritual and physical.

✝ It was an emblem that something new was taking place.

✝ It is contrary to the Greek text itself to treat this as a natural phenomenon. The presence of the conjunction *as* refutes any truth for the belief that this noise was a natural phenomenon. Nothing of such description could ever be a natural phenomenon.

As comes from the Greek conjunction ὥσπερ (ōspĕr) and demonstrates even more that this noise was not a natural phenomenon. Further, it also demonstrates that to all who heard this awesome noise, it sounded like a rushing, violent or mighty wind. The focus here by Luke is that this noise sounded like this, but actually was not. For Luke, this was the best manner of describing the noise. Literally, no true interpretation can describe this noise.

Luke actually uses three Greek words to describe this

noise. The first word that needs to be examined is the Greek noun πνοή (pnōē). This Greek noun is translated "wind."

According to Luke, the noise was so forceful and so inundated with the power of the Holy Spirit that as it moved instantaneously in the house it felt just like wind to those who were there. Notice that the physical senses can perceive the manifestation of the Holy Spirit.

The Greek adjective βίαιος (vēěŏs) here portrays the movement of this noise into the house as violent, forcible and even vehement. This was an illustration that the Holy Spirit was coming and coming in force and power. This is also a manifestation that the Holy Spirit was coming to battle against the forces that are against Him and the church. So, this Greek adjective shows that the war and battles against Satan would be renewed in fury and in power.

The Greek *present participle* φερομένη (fěrōměnē) is best translated "rushing" or "sweeping." This Greek participle causes the whole expression to be translated to "as of a mighty wind which is being rushed" or "as of rushing violent wind." The point here is that this Greek present participle is acting like another adjective and as such displays another characteristic of this noise. This noise was rushing, violent and "as wind." It describes the noise and shows that this noise is moving instantaneously from heaven to earth and especially in the upper room.

In addition, this Greek present participle is found in the *passive voice*. This indicates that the noise did not just occur by itself or by accident, but by divine prerogative.

According to the last part of verse two, the noise instantaneously filled most of the house where the apostles and all the others were sitting. This is understood from the Greek verb πληρόω (plērōō), and it is used in the momentary aorist.

While many believe that the entire house was filled by this noise, this is not the case. The Greek text does not mean *all*, but only a *considerable amount*. The purpose of Luke describing this is to show that the noise was only heard in the house where people were sitting. It did not fill any part in the house that did not have a person.

This shows that there was no lost motion in this operation. In other words, it shows that God does not waste time in efforts that will not be beneficial to His purpose and plans.

Before Acts 2 and in Acts 2, it is stated in several translations that all those who were present experienced all. However, this is not true. The Greek text clearly states the following according to Greek grammar and grammatical rules:

- ✞ Not all continued with one accord in prayer and supplication. (See Acts 1:8.)
- ✞ Not all on the Day of Pentecost were found in one accord in one place. (See Acts 2:1.)
- ✞ Not all of the house was filled with a noise from heaven. (See Acts 2:2.)
- ✞ Not all on the Day of Pentecost and in the same house were filled with the Holy Ghost, and neither did all speak in tongues. (See Acts 2:2, 7.)
- ✞ Not all marveled. (See Acts 2:7.)
- ✞ Not all were amazed. (See Acts 2:12.)

This is the case due to the Greek adjective πᾶς (päs) as well as the Greek adjective ὅλος (ōlōs)—each not having the article before them. When these adjectives do not have the article before them, they can only mean a "considerable amount."

Notice that the outpouring and the descent of the Holy Spirit were limited to just one house at the beginning. This structure was a house and not a temple. It was a house where the apostles and their contemporaries met. Arguments can be given to indicate that the place was even a private house:

✝ It is very unnatural to suppose that Luke meant a temple.

✝ The very language of the text does not even remotely denote such an interpretation.

✝ It was a private dwelling place—the one mentioned in Acts 1:13.

✝ It would be almost impossible for the Christian community on such a day as Pentecost to have been present in the temple for several hours.

✝ The assembling of the apostles and all others with them would have attracted public attention and the high priest and priests would have thrown them out because the apostles and all others with them were of the Christian community.

✝ There is no mention of the temple in Acts 1–2.

✝ The expression "the multitude came together," recorded in verse six, refutes that the apostles and their contemporaries were in the temple.

✝ The inauguration of the New Covenant being initialed in the official sanctuary, where the proclamation of the Old Covenant was made, is a contradiction that cannot be overcome. Why? There must not be a mixture of the Law and its rites with the gospel of grace and of faith.

ACTS 2:3

Acts 2:3 literally is translated from the Greek text as: "And there appeared instantaneously unto them tongues like as of fire being divided, and it sat instantaneously upon each of them."

Acts 2:3 describes the miracle wrought on the Day of Pentecost as a miracle of speech rather than hearing. It paints before the readers a peculiar feature of the outpouring and descent of the Holy Spirit. (See Acts 10:46; 19:6; Mark 16:17; 1 Corinthians 11:10.)

The Greek verb ὁράω (ōräō) is found in the passive voice and in the momentary aorist. The problem here is not the momentary aorist, but the passive voice. The passive voice here is almost impossible to express.

This Greek verb, functioning in the passive voice, means here that the tongues did not come about by chance, accident or spontaneous evolution. The passive voice means that God the Holy Spirit was directing and controlling the manifestations and coming of these tongues at this place and time. These tongues were being manifested by the Holy Spirit and came into the church by Him alone. He is the One who manifests this phenomenon. (See 1 Corinthians 12:4–7.)

From this verb one is also able to uncover that:

- ✝ The first occurrence of the gift of tongues by the New Testament saints is seen here.
- ✝ The gift of tongues appeared instantaneously to those who sought after them.
- ✝ There was no procession of them coming. They simply came instantaneously.

At best, this Greek verb in the passive tense is translated "there appeared," "there was appearing" or "there was being manifested."

This phenomenon was manifested to those in the upper room. (See Acts 1:13.) The action done by the Holy Spirit was for those in the upper room and no others at that time. Eventually, the whole world would experience this phenomenon.

The Greek noun γλῶσσα (glōsä) demands that the tongues themselves were genuine languages, not gibberish or sounds of foolishness. According to Greek grammar, the tongues mentioned are not the tongues of the individuals, but the languages that the individuals were being endowed with by the Holy Spirit.

The Greek *passive participle* διαμεριζόμενη (thēämĕrēzōmĕnē) cannot be translated "cloven." On the contrary, the idea here is that the tongues were being divided among those who sought to receive them. This phenomenon that appeared as fire was first in a single body in heaven.

However it became divided among those who sought to receive them. There is no indication by this Greek participle that all those present in the upper room received tongues nor that all those present in that upper room received all the tongues.

From this Greek participle, the tongues were obviously divided among those who sought to receive them. None received all languages but only one, two or several at this time as their permanent vehicle or manner of expressing this gift.

The Greek participle gives evidence that the Holy Spirit can, at His will, manifest any type of language through the believer at any time if the believer so permits. (See 1 Corinthians 14:32.) There is no limit noted by this participle.

The very thought of this Greek passive participle is more powerful than once thought by Greek scholars. It is all encompassing. The problem with those who have studied the practice of speaking in tongues is that they have forgotten the power of this participle. The Greek passive participle places the Holy Spirit in the midst of all types of communication that require speech. He is seen as the One who divides all these types into ways of manifesting the gift of tongues. This participle also includes not only all languages, but also all dialects.

Herein lies the problem. The very use of this Greek participle here may be in variance against Acts 2:5–15. Are the tongues only human that were manifested on the Day of Pentecost? Probably not. The evidence that angelic languages and the divine language were manifested on the Day of Pentecost with that of human languages is seen by the following arguments:

✝ The Greek passive participle supports that the angelic languages and the divine language had outbursts here, but not as forceful as human languages and dialects.

✝ The same Greek participle supports the idea of

the manifestation of a multiplicity of languages and dialects with no limit.

✟ If only human languages were represented in Acts 2, then the power of the Greek passive participle is lost. There would be no sense of the Holy Spirit dividing the languages so forcefully.

✟ The emphasis in Acts 2:8–15 is that of human language as a whole, but not completely.

✟ There are indications in thought within Acts 2:8–15 that give evidence that human languages were not alone in this incident.

✟ It is grammatically wrong to limit any type of language.

✟ The tongues spoken on the Day of Pentecost must have included that of angelic languages and even the divine language. For there would be no occasion for scorn if unknown human languages were spoken intelligibly. (See Acts 2:11–13.)

✟ The onlookers heard some languages that sounded unintelligible. These were languages and dialects that helped the onlookers conclude that the apostles and their contemporaries were drunk with wine. These languages must have been angelic and divine.

✟ The words "in Judæa" make it impossible for all the languages and dialects spoken at Pentecost to be only human. As such, it places within Judæa the manifestation of angelic and divine languages with human languages.

✟ The human languages take the forefront in the English translations, but the Greek text indicates the presence of other nonhuman languages.

✟ The forms of this phenomenon, recorded in verses 2 and 4, are comprehensive statements that nonhuman languages were manifested here.

✟ It is true that the Greek noun γλῶσσα (glōsä) is understood to denote the same as the Greek

noun διάλεκτος (thēälěktōs). However, this does
not disprove that angelic or divine languages
were also manifested on the Day of Pentecost.

The early church saw all forms of languages used by
the Holy Spirit in the gift of tongues.[1] They saw, at least in
the early times before Augustine, all types of languages
used in the gift of tongues, including those that are not
human, but angelic and divine.

In the work titled *Didache*, which was completed no
later than A.D. 120, it is said that those who speak in the
Spirit do so with languages that cannot be limited just to
human.[2]

The tongues are said to be "as of fire." This expression
describes the tongues as fiery tongues. Consequently,
Luke states that these tongues are fiery because they have
come with the anointing and power of the Holy Spirit, with
the Holy Spirit Himself, with a revival, and with an
emphasis on the ownership of believers. The "fire" is an
emblem of the gift of tongues.

The description of the tongues by Luke cannot be a
physical phenomenon. They must be a supernatural phenomenon. The appearance of fire was not seen physically
by the eyes of the onlookers, but through visions. By these
visions the onlookers, and those who were experiencing
this phenomenon, could see in the supernatural realm and
behold the power and glory of God. While the noise was
truly audible and heard by the ears of those in Jerusalem,
this phenomenon was restricted to the supernatural realm
and only manifested in that realm through visions.

The expression "as of fire" and the expressions in
Daniel 10:6 and in Revelation 1:14 all convey the same
thought. The appearance of all three could be observed
only in the supernatural realm by a vision. The appearance resembled that of natural fire, but it was not. It was
supernatural fire that appeared.

It was not the tongues themselves nor the Spirit
Himself who rested on the heads of each present, but the

appearance of fire on their heads. In other words, all those who were given permission to see this phenomenon by visions saw their heads lit up as a flame of fire. What a glorious phenomenon!

ACTS 2:4

Verse 4 literally is translated from the Greek text as, "And almost all were being filled instantaneously with the Holy Spirit, and they began to speak with other tongues, as the Spirit gave to them utterance."

Ordinarily, scholars and writers confess that all those found in the upper room were being filled instantaneously with the Holy Spirit. However, the Greek adjective πάς (päs) does not have the article before it. This demands that this Greek adjective can only mean a "considerable amount." Because of this, not all in the upper room were filled with the Holy Spirit.

The reason was that one, two or more willed not to be filled or resisted the Holy Spirit. The very fact that the Greek text does not indicate the totality of them being filled with the Holy Spirit shows free will permits the working of the Holy Spirit in one's life and that the Holy Spirit can be resisted in His work. That is one reason why Paul tells the believers not to grieve the Holy Spirit. (See Ephesians 4:30.) The Holy Spirit is never inactive, but always works wherever He dwells.

It is evident from the Greek text that some in the upper room did not receive the baptism and filling of the Holy Spirit, nor did they speak in tongues. Why? Though the Holy Spirit wanted all to be baptized and filled as a result of baptism, as well as to speak in tongues, some of the people resisted the Holy Spirit and His desire for the Christian church.

That a person can resist the Holy Spirit is clear from all the sin, rebellion and apostasy that exists. Notice Genesis 6:1–4. What Christ foretold in Mark 16:17–18 came true at the very onset of the descent of the Holy Spirit.

All that has been said about the very practice of speaking in tongues, as witnessed by the Book of Acts, is rejected by those who limit the whole Book of Acts to a historical sense. The argument follows like this: "Acts is a historical narrative, not an instructive and doctrinal narrative. The Book of Acts is a record of the early church's experiences that does not deal with instructions for believers throughout the church age. The epistles of Paul are more in line with an instructive and doctrinal narrative."

This thinking is wholly false in its foundation because of the arguments that follow:

- ✞ Acts is a representation of the apostolic faith in word and deed. To deny that the Book of Acts has any instructive or doctrinal importance is highly unethical and unbiblical.

- ✞ Limiting the book to only a historical sense, apart from any instructive or doctrinal importance, is separating the modern church from the apostolic faith and making the faith of modern times something other than the apostolic faith.

- ✞ If the same system of interpretation is followed throughout the Bible, all books that deal with a historical narrative—such as Genesis, Exodus, Leviticus, Numbers, Deuteronomy, Judges and others—must be dismissed as having any importance for instruction and doctrine. However, all these books contain important instructions and important doctrines throughout the historical narrative. Do we dismiss the doctrine of creation, the doctrine of God, the doctrine of the trinity, the doctrine of angels, the doctrine of evil, the doctrine of omnipresence, the doctrine of omnipotence, the doctrine of redemption, the doctrine of Messiah and other doctrines when they are found in such books? God forbid! When these books bear witness to a doctrine, it is quoted, discussed and given as proof of such a doctrine being practiced and believed by the Christian church.

✝ It's true that the historical accounts of the
process of the early church must be said to compose the contents of the book, but the book itself
cannot be dismissed as only a historical narrative. In addition, it represents in its construction
a chronicle of divine and human origin because
it sets forth the authority of Christ, the working
of the Holy Spirit in signs and wonders, and the
experience of His apostles and His church.
Accordingly, the Book of Acts is a witness of the
apostolic faith in its true form; a guide for
church government; a book of rules and disci-
pline for the church; a storehouse of weapons
against the spirit of Antichrist; an arsenal of
weapons against all the errors and heresies of
our faith; a storehouse that promotes the very
nourishment of our faith, patience and hope;
and a treasure house of sound doctrine.

The very expression "speak in other tongues" has been
anciently interpreted to denote "genuine languages other
than those that one knows, has learned or is acquainted
with." This very phrase is a sign that the gospel speaks with
a tongue that is set on fire and flaming.

Speaking in tongues follows a pattern and includes all
the functions of a working grammar. Though sometimes
the sounds or pronunciations of genuine speaking in
tongues may not seem to be a language, it is because a language is used on these occasions beyond human compre-
hension to recognize a pattern or even a type of grammar.

Genuine speaking in tongues cannot be what is commonly called ecstatic utterance. Ecstatic utterance is
pagan and not what was experienced on the Day of
Pentecost. Ecstatic utterance suggests that the person who
is practicing speaking in tongues is insane and has lost
control of himself.

As such, ecstatic utterance means a state of being
beyond reason and self-control. Paul made clear that
speaking in tongues was not beyond reason, self-control
or the will of the saint. (See 1 Corinthians 14:27–28.)

What has been forgotten by those who are against speaking in tongues is the fact that if there are genuine tongues, then there are also false tongues.

There are, in fact, four types of counterfeit tongues:

☩ Those tongues that are spoken by demons through a human agent.

☩ Tongues that either are unconnected sounds that make no sense but have become learned behavior or vain repetitions of words. (See Matthew 6:7.)

☩ Psychological tongues that originate only from mental illness and are not connected to demon possession or demon activity.

☩ Pathological tongues that originate from the effects of drugs or other types of organic neurological damage.

Observe that Paul saw for genuine Christians no need for concern or fear over counterfeit tongues, even in the city of Corinth, which was a very pagan city. (See 1 Corinthians 10:20; 14:2.) Paul argued against a genuine Christian receiving a counterfeit tongue, due to the Holy Spirit's powerful work in the lives of believers. (See 1 Corinthians 12:3.)

Paul uses 1 Corinthians 12:3 as reassurance that demonic worship, pagan worship or even an alien practice cannot influence, much less corrupt, the genuine spiritual gifts of the Holy Spirit. He believed the Corinthians were speaking in genuine tongues, only that they were misusing them. First Corinthians 12–14 sees the gift of tongues as a good gift that has a value for believers.

The reports of demons speaking in other tongues through people are actually the works of Satan, who is trying to destroy the genuine gift of tongues. Paul encouraged speaking in tongues. Such reports are orchestrated by Satan to discourage speaking in tongues. Satan will use all his designs, such as lying, to achieve this.

Notice that Satan hates speaking in tongues. Why? It is

the only type of communication used now by man that he cannot hinder, corrupt, listen to, understand or stop. (See 1 Corinthians 14:2; Romans 8:26.)

The possibility that Satan can counterfeit the gifts of the Holy Spirit for unbelievers is seen in Matthew 7:22–24, John 10:10 and Ephesians 5:11. However, it is impossible that Satan can counterfeit the gifts of the Holy Spirit for believers who remain genuine and stay out of a state of lukewarmness, continue to manifest positive fruits in their lives, and continue to manifest positive fruits from the gifts of the Holy Spirit. (See 1 Corinthians 12:3; 1 John 4:4; Matthew 7:16–20.)

Appropriately, genuine Christians do not manifest counterfeit gifts. Those who do are deceived, have become lukewarm or backsliders, and may even be demon-possessed unbelievers. Do not let experience interpret and test the Scripture. Rather, let Scripture interpret and test experience.

The Greek infinitive λαλεῖν (lälēn) is generally used to show that all the tongues spoken were nothing but human languages. However, the Greek infinitive λαλεῖν (lälēn) cannot be limited in such a way. It is true that this Greek infinitive can represent speech of a human origin and deals with human languages. (See Matthew 12:22, 34; Mark 7:37; 12:1; Luke 7:15; John 8:26; Acts 4:17, 20; 5:40; 11:15; 1 Corinthians 14:34–39; 1 Thessalonians 1:8.) Yet, this Greek infinitive can also represent speech that occurred supernaturally. (See Luke 4:41; Mark 1:34; Exodus 34:29.)

Because this Greek infinitive does represent what occurs supernaturally, there can be no limit to the method of speaking chosen by the Holy Spirit.

Furthermore, the Greek verb λαλέω (lälĕō) is used to express that the Holy Spirit does speak. (See Matthew 10:20.) Because the Holy Spirit is not limited in His manner of communication, and even can use imperfect ways to communicate (which are all forms of speech), then the Greek verb λαλέω (lälĕō)—whether used as a conjugated verb or in the infinitive—cannot be limited just to human languages. It must be all-inclusive. The Greek passive participle in verse 3 causes the Greek infinitive to be all-inclusive.

The Greek adjective ἕτερος (ĕtĕrōs), as in Mark 16:17–18, does not prove that the tongues are only angelic, but all-inclusive.

Furthermore, the expression "with other tongues" shows that those who experienced this phenomenon were transported from the physical realm to that of the supernatural realm. They no longer spoke their own language, but the Holy Spirit spoke through them by means of tongues. In other words, the tongues were not their own, yet tongues were being spoken only under the influence, persuasion and control of the Holy Spirit.

From the phrase "as the Spirit gave to them utterance," one is able to understand that the Holy Spirit throughout all of this repeatedly and continually gave to these believers the ability to speak in tongues. It came from no other source! When the Holy Spirit draws away His power, the utterance stops.

The *imperfect tense* used in this phrase means that all those who spoke in tongues did so as a group. Compare this with 1 Corinthians 14:23. The *imperfect tense* does not state that everyone who spoke in tongues continued and did not stop at all, but that they continued as a group while some individuals stopped speaking in tongues and only began again when the Holy Spirit gave them the utterance to do so. The gift of tongues comes and goes, like waves of the sea, as the Spirit gives men the power of utterance.

Nonetheless, some will point out that all who were speaking in tongues on the Day of Pentecost stopped when Peter began to proclaim a message in his native tongue. (See Acts 2:11–14.) The Greek text refutes this undeniably.

Acts 2:14 reads, "But Peter, standing with the eleven, lifted up." From the Greek text, which uses a Greek *aorist participle,* several things are understood:

> ✝ The apostles were standing together at the same time that others were doubting, questioning and mocking the practice of speaking in tongues.

> ✝ Speaking in tongues was still continuing even though Peter, under the guidance and influence of the Holy Spirit, ceased proclaiming what was going on.

> ✝ The apostles as a whole had not ceased speaking in tongues at this time.

> ✝ The only one of the twelve apostles that had ceased under the direct command of the Holy Spirit was Peter.

Within the Greek text of Acts 2:14, a circumstantial clause is used. It deals with contemporaneous action. What does this mean? That the doubting, questioning, mocking and standing up of the twelve and speaking in tongues all were going on at the same time. There is no question about it.

In Acts 2, there is neither an orderly succession of individual speakers nor even an overriding concern for the speakers. The speaking in tongues on the Day of Pentecost, as recorded in verse 11, only consisted of the praises of God and His wonderful works. Here, the speaking in tongues is not for preaching as is commonly believed. It for manifesting the wonderful works of God. (See Acts 2:11.)

In Acts 2:4, the Greek verb ἀποφθέγγομαι (äpōfthĕngōmĕ) means "utterance; to speak out loudly and clearly; the ability to speak; to speak with emphasis; to be under the control or influence of the divine; to be transported into the spiritual realm to see visions or to speak with tongues supplied supernaturally to the receiver."

The ancients have seen this verb as evidence that the gift of tongues is more—much more—than just human languages.

The high point of the use of this Greek verb is that most

of the approximately one hundred twenty people at the Day of Pentecost gave consent from their own wills to be raptured into the spiritual realm and endowed with abilities that were directed and under the control of the Spirit.

Further, this Greek verb is found in the Greek text in an infinitive form. From this, the infinitive sets forth the absolute truth and fact that the gift of tongues is not directed, worked or even operated by the will of the believer but by the will of the Holy Spirit. It is He alone who gives and even continues to give the ability and capacity to speak in tongues.

The Greek verb ἀποφθέγγομαι (äpōfthĕngōmĕ) is used in the Greek Septuagint five times exclusively with the oracular speech of true and false prophets. Suggested by its use is some strange style of speech that includes the genuine and counterfeit tongues. (See 1 Chronicles 25:1; Ezekiel 13:9, 19; Micah 5:11; Zechariah 10:2.)

There is much similarity here. One should notice that the fervor of the prophets, who by yielding themselves to the power of the Holy Spirit and yet retaining self-control, is seen to include broken cries and strange unintelligible speech that is not known by the speaker but is known somewhere. (See Numbers 11:25; 12:6–8; 1 Samuel 10:5–6; 19:20–21; 1 Kings 18:28–29; 2 Kings 9:11.)

All these passages prove conclusively that among the prophets there existed the practice of speaking in tongues, though to an inferior degree. All these passages do not prove that all prophets experienced this phenomenon, nor that the ones who did were robbed of their self-consciousness or their self-control. They prove that they were in a state of passive receptivity. (See 1 Corinthians 14:32.)[3]

While Paul recognizes that speaking in tongues is also found in heathen religions, there are similarities and parallels between what is practiced in Christianity and what is practiced by the heathens. Paul sees a distinction between the Christian experience and the heathen experience. (See 1 Corinthians 12:2.)

Paul does not trace this phenomenon back to the mysticism of the heathens, but to the ancient prophets of the Old Testament—like all astute Jews at that time, versed in knowledge about the prophets, would have done. Peter even traces the phenomenon of speaking in tongues on the Day of Pentecost not back to the heathens but back to Joel, one of the prophets. (See Joel 2:28–29.) In addition, Luke goes further and states that speaking in tongues by the gift of tongues has a heavenly origin. (See Acts 2:2.)

Undoubtedly, Luke, by stating that the tongues manifested on the Day of Pentecost were of a heavenly origin, denies that the heathen experience of speaking in tongues is the same as what occurred on Pentecost. He additionally states that speaking in tongues by the prophets and other Old Testament saints on occasion was not the same as the experience that occurred on the Day of Pentecost.

While the source is the same, the speaking in tongues that occurred on occasion by the prophets and other Old Testament saints came about not through the gift of tongues, but through the Holy Spirit endowing a person with the ability to speak in other languages apart from the gift of tongues. The difference between the Old Testament experience and the New Testament experience is that in the New Testament experience speaking in tongues is governed under the gift of tongues and in the Old Testament experience speaking in tongues was governed under the gift of prophecy.

In 1 Enoch 71:11, Enoch is said to cry with a loud voice and with the spirit of power. It is taken here that Enoch spoke in strange speech or spoke in tongues.

In Daniel 4:16–19, according to the Greek Septuagint, it is believed that Daniel was in the Spirit and spoke before the king in a strange unintelligible tongue for about an hour. This was a manifestation of what would occur on the Day of Pentecost.

In Daniel 5:5, especially—according to the Greek Septuagint—the writing on the wall is seen as unintelligible language that could not be understood except by Daniel. The reason was that the language written on the wall was of angelic origin.

One of the greatest critics of the Scriptures and of Christianity was a man by the name of Celsus who lived in the second and third centuries. Celsus accused the Old Testament prophets and the Christian prophets as prophesying in the same manner and with the same strange unintelligible speech that the ancient heathen prophets used. Origen refuted this and presented that while there are some similarities, the speech was not the same, nor is the source the same, nor was even the manner in which the prophecy came forth.[4]

Celsus renders one clear proof that the ancient heathens spoke in their own form of tongues long before the dawning of Christianity. Celsus states:

> To these promises are added strange, fanatical, and quite unintelligible words, of which no rational person can find the meaning; for so dark are they, as to have no meaning at all; but they give occasion to every fool or imposter to apply them to suit his own purposes.[5]

Irenæus sees no difference between Hellenistic prophecy and the prophecy that came from a woman who was one of the Christian occultists following the Gnostic heresy.[6]

Origen, comparing the heathen prophets with those glorious prophets in the Old Testament, declares:

> These, and a multitude of others prophesying on behalf of God, foretold events relating to Jesus Christ. We therefore for this reason set at nought the oracles of the Pythian priestess, or those delivered at Dodona, at Clarus, at Banchidæ, at the temple of Jupiter Ammon or by a multitude of other so called prophets whilst we regard with reverent awe the Jewish prophets: for we see that the noble, earnest, and devout lives of these

men were worthy of the inspiration of the Divine
Spirit, whose wonderful effects were widely different from the divination of demons.[7]

The Greek text of Acts 2:4 refutes the concept that any of
the languages bestowed by the Holy Spirit became the prop-
erty of the individuals—with no place for the Holy Spirit in
their operation. The Greek text of that verse places the Holy
Spirit in the midst of all their operation and shows that the
Spirit is the One who gives the utterance of these languages. The event mentioned here in Acts 2:1–15 is a
sudden and powerful inspiration of the Holy Spirit by which
those present on the Day of Pentecost uttered the praises of
God, not of their mind, but as the mouthpiece of the Holy
Spirit in various languages.

Yet, it may be objected that if this is so, then those who
spoke in tongues could not understand what they said.
This is truly the case as seen from 1 Corinthians 14, for
speaking in tongues was found to be used where none
could interpret them.

This is also the case as seen by Peter's speech. Peter
himself did not understand what was said. For only
hearers said that what was spoken of were the "wonderful
works of God." (See Acts 2:11.)

The tongues were used as an instrument not for
teaching and preaching, but for praises unto the gracious
God who goes to the utmost to save. In other words, the
tongues manifested within the incident of Acts 2 were
never for the purpose of teaching and preaching the
gospel of Christ.

Indeed, there is no trace at all in Acts 2 that the tongues
manifested were for teaching and preaching the gospel.
This train of thought runs contrary to the whole course of
Scripture and early patristic evidence on the subject.
Therefore, modern thought about tongues is rejected as
wholly false.

In addition to this, there is no trace at all of such a
power or ability being possessed by those present on the

Day of Pentecost or afterward by the apostle Paul.

It should be noted that Paul was endowed with the gift of tongues, yet he could not understand the human speech of Lycaonia. (See 1 Corinthians 14:18; Acts 14:11–14.) That the apostles could not preach the gospel in all languages is witnessed as so by Papias, an ancient leader of the church. This man knew the apostles and never saw this supposed ability firsthand.[8]

The only possible early patristic evidence before A.D. 202 that suggests the gift of tongues was for the preaching of the gospel is found in an obscure passage of the ancient father Irenæus who lived in the second century.

A translation of the Latin text follows:

> Who also, Luke says, descended after the ascension of the Lord upon the disciples at the day of Pentecost, having power over all nations for the entrance of life, and for the defense of the New Testament; from which place also, they proclaimed, united in all languages, a song of praise to God, the Spirit bringing different tribes into unity, and offering to the Father the first-fruits of all nations.[9]

No one can prove, much less convince, any that Irenæus taught that the apostles and others there at the Day of Pentecost were endowed with the supernatural ability to speak and understand all human languages for the purpose of preaching the gospel. Certainly, according to the Latin text, the apostles are not said, by Irenæus, to have power over all nations for the purpose of the entrance of life or for the renewal of spiritual life through the blood of Christ but the Holy Spirit.

According to the Latin text, Irenæus sees the descent of the Holy Spirit as the purpose for bringing people into the state of redemption and for the purpose of defending the New Testament. This is seen by Latin text tying together the Latin words *quem* and *habentem* in the singular number and in the accusative case. In the Latin text, the term *disciple* is in the plural number and in the accusative case. This indicates a clear difference between the Holy Spirit and the apostles.

In the thinking of Irenæus, he saw a division: some apostles speaking earthly languages, others speaking angelic languages, some speaking the divine language.

Also, Irenæus does not state that the disciples each received every human language. Rather, they all together were able to give at least one example of every kind and species of language that there is. This opens the door to the belief that at least one apostle (or even more) spoke in languages that were not of this world.

Further, one should notice that Irenæus says that the tongues were a "song of praise" to God, not a sermon to the onlookers nor a means of teaching and preaching the Word of God or the message of Christ coming to save humanity from their sins. Therefore, speaking in tongues is not about preaching.

There was never a commission by Jesus Christ for the apostles themselves (or any other) to preach the gospel message to the entire world. Matthew 28:19 does not contain a commission by which the apostles (and others) are ordered to preach the gospel to every nation in the world.

The absence of the article before the Greek adjective for *all* indicates what the Lord commanded was for the apostles (and others) to go preach the gospel to many nations. It is a fact that the apostles (and others) in the first century fulfilled this. This has been repeatedly fulfilled by Christians throughout the centuries.

Because the Roman Empire comprised many nations, if the apostles (and others) had preached the gospel only within the empire, the commission would have been so fulfilled. However, they preached the gospel to other nations that were not part of the empire and even went beyond fulfilling this commission.

This has been said in order to show that the apostles and Christians in the first century were able to fulfill this commission easily by simply using the universal language of that time—Greek—and for some time later. It was the official language of the Roman Empire. It was all one needed to know to carry out all types of commerce within the empire.

Notice that what most of the people in the upper room experienced brought rebuke and mocking. Further, they were accused mainly by native Jews of being drunk with wine.

The order of the words in Acts 2:15, "Not as ye suppose are these drunken," signifies that those in the upper room were truly drunk, but by the sweet wine of gladness presented by Christ through the Holy Spirit. The very use of the conjunction demands that Luke saw a comparison between two states of drunkenness.

The first state was of the Holy Spirit. The second state was of wine. Notice that "new wine" in Acts 2:13 is not newly made wine, which is not intoxicating, but new sweet wine, which is very intoxicating.

The early church interpreted this passage to mean that they were so intoxicated with the power of God that they physically acted like they were drunk. The early church saw being drunk in the Spirit as a fulfillment of Psalm 36:8. Tertullian taught that those who were drunk were deemed drunkards by all those who saw them.[10]

Those present to see this spectacle were Jews among the nations and Gentile proselytes. (See Acts 2:9–11.) The Jews who witnessed this spectacle have been divided into four main divisions:

> ✝ Eastern or Babylonian, such as the Parthians, Medes, Elamites and Mesopotamians. These Jews were the descendants of Jews that were in the Assyrian captivity and the Babylonian captivity.

> ✝ Syrian, such as those from Judea, Cappadocia, Pontus, Asia, Phrygia and Pamphylia. These Jews were the descendants of the ones who were in the Syrian captivity instigated by Antiochus IV Epiphanes.

✠ Egyptian, such as those from Egypt, Libya or
Cyrene. These Jews were the descendants of the
ones who were planted by Ptolemy I, Soter.

✠ Roman Jews.

Acts 10:44–46, Acts 19:6 and Acts 11:15 cannot be given
to prove that the manifestations of tongues in Acts 2 were
limited to human languages. On the contrary, Acts
10:44–46 is a general statement of the supernatural utterance of the Holy Spirit through men. Yet, the vaguest
brush by Luke exhibits that in this example languages
other than human ones were present.

Notice that the people heard tongues but could not
define what was said. They heard something, but they
could not understand it. Within the Greek text, the Greek
thought permeates that all languages were being spoken.
The Greek thought is all-inclusive.

Neither is there any limit to what type of tongues were
spoken at Ephesus, as witnessed by Greek grammar. (See
Acts 19:6.) The episode of the Holy Spirit falling on those
in the house of Cornelius in Acts 11:15 was very similar to
that of Acts 2. And it has been shown that the tongues
manifested there were not just human.

In summary, the most common mistake about inter-
preting Acts 2 is to conclude that it deals only with human
languages. The facts are that other languages different
from human languages were also present. These facts
come from Greek thought, context, content and syntax.

Overview of Chapter Three

Acts 2:2

1. The phrase "there came" indicates that something new was coming. It was a new state of
Christian experience.

2. The *momentary aorist* indicates that the new
experience was instantaneous in its coming.

3. The word *suddenly* indicates that this immediate, instantaneous and spontaneous incident

was a shock and a surprise to those who were assembled on the Day of Pentecost.

4. The phenomenon mentioned in Acts 2:2 originated not from the earth but from heaven itself.

5. In Acts 2:2, the word *noise* may be described in several ways:

✞ Heavenly

✞ Frightening

✞ Amazing

✞ Bewildering

✞ It caused those who heard it to turn their attention to it.

✞ It was the very noise of heaven in all its glory and with all its faculties.

✞ It was heard by all of God's angels, all of the satanic forces and all those who were in Jerusalem.

✞ It transcended the spiritual realm and entered the physical realm.

✞ It was such a noise that all who had an ear could hear it.

✞ It was a noise that indicated a new experience for the Christian.

✞ It was a noise that indicated a new walk for the Christian, a walk in the Spirit.

✞ It was such an awesome noise that it indicated the coming of the Holy Spirit in all His fullness in this life.

✞ It was chosen by the Holy Spirit as the best vehicle through which He should come.

✞ It was an external manifestation.

✞ Nothing like this had ever occurred before. It is as if this "noise" of heaven had been held back until this special time.

✞ It was the noise of the herald proclaiming the arrival of the Holy Spirit.

✝ It was the indication that the limitation of the Holy Spirit would be brought to an end and the beginning of the fullness of the Holy Spirit would begin.

✝ Also, it was the very demonstration that God Himself was fulfilling His promise of the Comforter, coming and outpouring Himself through the baptism.

✝ What was heard was the very breathing or blowing of the Holy Spirit.

✝ It accompanied the descent of the Holy Spirit and echoed throughout all of creation.

✝ So awesome was this noise that it shook the very foundations of hell.

✝ It was a demonstration again that Satan had failed.

✝ It was truly a noise and truly audible.

✝ The noise was so loud that it was heard throughout Jerusalem.

✝ This noise was of such a nature that it could well be heard n both realms.

✝ It was an emblem that something new was taking place.

✝ The phenomenon mentioned in Acts 2:2 was not natural but supernatural.

6. The noise was moving into the house as a violent, forcible and even vehement wind.

7. The noise is an illustration that the Holy Spirit was coming in force and power.

8. Not all the house was filled with the noise.

9. The house was a private house, not a temple, because:

✝ It is very unnatural to suppose that Luke meant a temple.

✝ The language of the text does not even remotely denote such an interpretation.

✟ It was a private dwelling place, the one mentioned in Acts 1:13.

✟ It would have been almost impossible for the Christian community to have been present in the temple for several hours on such a day as Pentecost.

✟ The assembling of the apostles and all others with them would have attracted public attention, and the high priest and priests would have thrown them out because the apostles and all others with them were of the Christian community.

✟ There is no mention of the temple in Acts 1 and 2.

✟ The expression "the multitude came together," recorded in verse 6, refutes that the apostles and their contemporaries were in the temple.

✟ That the inauguration of the New Covenant would have been initialed in the official sanctuary and proclamation site of the Old Covenant is a contradiction that cannot be overcome.

Acts 2:3

1. The miracle mentioned in Acts 2:3 was one of speech rather than hearing.

2. From the Greek text, it is seen that the Holy Spirit was directing and controlling the manifestations and coming of these tongues at this place and time.

3. It is also uncovered from the Greek text that:

    ✟ The first occurrence of the gift of tongues by the New Testament saints is seen here.

    ✟ The gift of tongues appeared instantaneously.

    ✟ There was no procession of them coming. They simply came instantaneously.

4. The phenomenon was manifested to those who were in the upper room first. (See Acts 1:13.)

5. From the Greek text, it is learned that tongues

were genuine languages, not gibberish or sounds of foolishness.

6. The tongues were in a single body in heaven, but became divided among those who sought to receive them.

7. Greek grammar gives evidence that the Holy Spirit can, at His will, manifest any type of language through the believer.

8. Greek grammar indicates that angelic languages and the divine language were manifested on the Day of Pentecost with human languages.

9. The early church saw all forms of languages used by the Holy Spirit in the gift of tongues.

10. The tongues being like fire symbolizes:
    ♱ The anointing of the Holy Spirit
    ♱ The Holy Spirit
    ♱ Revival
    ♱ Ownership by believers
    ♱ The power of the Holy Spirit

11. The appearance of fire was what lighted on the heads of those in the upper room.

12. The appearance of fire was seen by onlookers, not physically but through visions. It was supernatural.

Acts 2:4

1. Not all were filled with the Holy Spirit in the upper room, according to Greek grammar.

2. The Greek text does not indicate the totality of persons being filled with the Holy Spirit.

3. The argument that the Book of Acts is limited to a historical sense and therefore what occurred on the Day of Pentecost only occurred with the

apostolic church is wholly false. The arguments are given in the last chapter.

4. The phrase "speak in other tongues" has anciently been interpreted to denote "genuine languages other than those that one knows, has learned or is acquainted with."

5. Speaking in tongues follows a pattern and includes all the functions of a working grammar.

6. Genuine speaking in tongues is not ecstatic utterance.

7. There are four types of counterfeit tongues:
   ☦ Tongues spoken by demons through a human agent
   ☦ Tongues that are either unconnected sounds that make no sense and have become a learned behavior or vain repetitions of words
   ☦ Psychological tongues
   ☦ Pathological tongues

8. There is no concern or fear over counterfeit tongues for those who are genuine Christians.

9. The reports of demons speaking in other tongues through people are actually the workings of Satan to destroy the genuine gift of tongues.

10. The possibility that Satan can counterfeit the gifts of the Holy Spirit for unbelievers is seen in Matthew 7:22–24 and John 10:10.

11. The phrase "with other tongues" shows that those who experienced this phenomenon were transported from the physical realm to the supernatural realm.

12. From the phrase "as the Spirit gave to them

utterance" we are able to understand that the Holy Spirit gave these believers the ability to speak in tongues.

13. In Acts 2 there is no orderly succession of individual speakers seen, nor even an overriding concern for the speakers.

14. The speaking in tongues on the Day of Pentecost, as recorded in verse 11, consisted only of the praises of God and His wonderful works.

15. In Acts 2:4, it is well established that the gift of tongues is not directed, worked or even operated by the will of the believer, but by the will of the Holy Spirit.

16. From Acts 2:4 it is seen that among the Old Testament prophets there existed the practice of speaking in tongues.

17. Historically, it is known that some of the Old Testament prophets spoke in tongues.

18. The apostles were so intoxicated with the power of God that they physically acted like they were drunk. (See Acts 2:13.)

19. There is no limit of what type of tongues were spoken at Ephesus, as witnessed by Greek grammar. (See Acts 19:6.)

Chapter Four

The Baptism
of the Holy Spirit

Since the Reformation there has been and continues to be an absolute quagmire about the experiences that Christians can face. Some demand that there is only one experience for Christians. Others state that there are two experiences, which are salvation and sanctification. Still others believe that there are three experiences—salvation, sanctification and the baptism of the Holy Spirit.

The limiting of experiences from the Lord to one, two or three is not blasphemous, but it is truly ridiculous. The Holy Spirit is omnipotent and cannot be limited to showing His might to His saints in one, two or three events. There are countless levels and deeper depths to the Holy Spirit than the saints can imagine.

There are glorious revelations, incidents and experiences that will bewilder the saints as they did the apostle Paul. He dared not speak about all his experiences fearing that doing so might bring forth confusion, bewilderment and doubt to the Christian community. In other words, Paul would have blown their minds by what God had shown him. Therefore, it is ridiculous to limit the Holy Spirit in His works and in the experiences that the saints can see.

The church has forgotten its place and, more importantly, the place of the Holy Spirit in the church. The teaching of the church about the baptism of the Holy Spirit, which is in vogue today, is an example of the church as a whole not knowing what the Holy Spirit can do and what a saint can experience from the Holy Spirit.

In particular, some today teach that the baptism of the Holy Spirit appeared in the Old Testament. The opposite is true. The baptism of the Holy Spirit, which will be defined shortly, must be unique and must be peculiarly the work of the Holy Spirit for the present age. It began for the church at the Day of Pentecost and continues for the church until she is caught away at Christ's coming.

Commonly, the view about the baptism of the Holy Spirit is that it is linked with other ministries of the Holy Spirit such as the indwelling of the Spirit, which is called regeneration. It is also seen to be coextensive with salvation. In other words, it is commonly held that every saint of God is baptized with the Holy Spirit at the point of salvation.

According to this view, it is impossible to be saved without being baptized with the Holy Spirit. In addition, this doctrine adds that the baptism into Christ and the baptism of the Holy Spirit are the same experience. From this viewpoint, it is held that because there is only one baptism, the baptism of the Holy Spirit and the baptism into Christ must be one and the same.

This idea has caused much damage within the church. It has disarmed the church and made it vulnerable to attack. The church, or all who will listen to this one view, have been robbed of their power. The church has become powerless and void of the supernatural gifts needed to offset the works of Satan. The suffering of the saints, at least in some respect, is present in the church that does not have the power as a whole to counteract the fiery darts of Satan.

Without understanding the true sense of what the baptism of the Holy Spirit is, it is impossible to rightly conceive what happened on the Day of Pentecost and how the gift of tongues is connected to that experience. The purpose of this chapter is to define what those in the upper room experienced and how the gift of tongues relates to what they experienced. Indeed, without having a clear grasp of this, the gift of tongues cannot be rightly understood.

THE FILLING AND THE BAPTISMS

The term "filled with the Holy Spirit" must be understood in the light of Greek studies and the views of the ancient church. From the Greek text itself it is clearly seen that the filling of the Holy Spirit cannot be the same as the baptism of the Holy Spirit. Neither can the baptism of the Holy Spirit be the same as the baptism into Christ.

Further, it shall be shown that there are differences between the filling and the baptism of the Holy Spirit. Notice that John the Baptist, Elizabeth and Zacharias experienced this blessing of filling, which was before the descent and outpouring of the Holy Spirit in the form of a baptism. (See Luke 1:15, 41, 67.)

In the Greek text, the phrases expressing the filling of John the Baptist, Elizabeth and Zacharias with the Holy Spirit are almost identical in construction and truly identical in thought, context, content and syntax with the phrase in Acts 2:4. In other words, the same event and phenomenon pertaining to the filling of the Holy Spirit are brought under discussion in both Luke 1 and Acts 2:4.

The Greek expression, πνεύματος ἁγίου (pněvmätōs äyēou), found in one form or another in Acts 2:4; 4:8, 31; 9:17; 13:9; 52:9; Luke 1:15, 41, 67 and Ephesians 5:18, denotes being filled with the Holy Spirit. This Greek expression is very complex. It expresses several constructions in one.

First, it is known in Greek as *the ablative of source, the ablative of means,* and *the genitive of cause.* All three of these Greek constructions are represented here. All these constructions show that the Holy Spirit alone is the cause, means and source of this experience. Also, this Greek expression is known in Greek as *the genitive of relationship, connection, association, union* and *membership.*

Here, those who are filled with the Holy Spirit are seen

to be in a relationship with Him and enjoy the benefits of such a relationship as this, but only in measure.

Further, the people united to the Holy Spirit witness His power, glory, blessings, gifts and other graces in their lives, but only in measure. Also, people are not filled literally with the person of the Holy Spirit but with His power, glory, blessings and other graces.

However, for this union to be full in this life, the baptism of the Holy Spirit must be experienced by a believer. "Filling" is only a measure of these things, and some things may not be manifested until the baptism is experienced.

The baptism of the Holy Spirit is generally written not in the genitive or ablative cases but in the *locative* and *instrumental* cases. This indicates a difference between the filling and baptism of the Holy Spirit. Notice that Acts 1:5 uses the locative and instrumental cases to describe the baptism. Acts 2:4 uses the genitive and ablative cases to describe the filling. This definitely shows a difference even in the mind of Luke.

The Greek verb βαπτίζω (väptĕzō) in these passages cannot be the same as filling. The filling itself, mentioned in Acts 2:4, cannot be seen as the promise of the Comforter to baptize believers with the Holy Spirit, but it must be seen as the result of such baptism. (See Acts 1:4–11; 11:15; Luke 24:49; Matthew 18:18; John 1:31–33; 7:38–39; 14:12–17.) Therefore, the promise of baptism with the Holy Spirit is far more than just being filled with the Holy Spirit. The Old Testament saints experienced being filled with the Holy Spirit, but none experienced being baptized with that same Holy Spirit. (See Exodus 28:3; 31:3; 35:31–35; Micah 3:8; Luke 1:15–17, 41, 67.) Even the apostles were filled with the Holy Spirit before the Day of Pentecost. (See John 14:17; 20:22; Mark 6:7–13; Luke 10:1–18.)

Many saints never experienced the baptism of the Holy Spirit. Also, notice that others were filled with the Holy Spirit before Pentecost but were never baptized with the Holy Spirit. (See Luke 1:41–67; 2:25–28.) Jesus Himself was filled with the Holy Spirit from birth. (See Isaiah 50:4–5; Luke 2:40, 52.) However, He was not baptized with the Holy Spirit until the Holy Spirit came upon Him in the form of a dove at His baptism in water. (See Matthew 3:16–17; 20:22–23; John 3:34; Luke 4:16–21; Acts 10:38; Isaiah 11:2; 42:1–5; 61:1–2.) Only then was Jesus endowed with the gifts of the Holy Spirit.

Further, the filling mentioned in Acts 2:4 was the result of the baptism that occurred almost instantaneously. Most of those in the upper room experienced the baptism of the Holy Spirit and the filling of the Holy Spirit, but not all of them. Paul also experienced almost instantaneously the baptism and filling of the Holy Spirit together, according to Greek thought. (See Acts 9:17.)

What is the difference between being filled with the Holy Spirit and being baptized with the Holy Spirit? The filling of the Holy Spirit is in essence receiving the Holy Spirit in measure, and the baptism of the Holy Spirit is in essence receiving the Holy Spirit in His fullness. The baptism of the Holy Spirit may also be defined as the immersion of the believer in the Holy Spirit so that the believer receives the fullness of the Holy Spirit and by this is endowed with power for service.

The Old Testament saints received the Holy Spirit in measure, not in His fullness. (See Numbers 11:16–25; 1 Kings 17:1–2; 2 Kings 2:9; 13:21; James 5:17; Luke 1:15–17.) Even the apostles received the Holy Spirit in measure before the Day of Pentecost.

In short, the filling and baptism may be simply defined as the Holy Spirit with (in or by) measure and the Holy Spirit without measure.

The baptism of the Holy Spirit, then, is a different experience from salvation or conversion. This fact, among other facts, leads to the conclusion that the new wine referred to in Acts 2:13 required new wineskins that were already made a new creation through the message of the gospel. (See Matthew 9:17.)

Consequently, the baptism of the Holy Spirit must come after, whether immediately or sometime later. Why? The new wine cannot be poured into an old wineskin that has not already gone through a transformation by the grace of God and through faith in Jesus Christ.

Let it be known that the baptism of the Holy Spirit opens the door to many great and wonderful things. Yet, it does not concern holiness. It is not the same as the fruits of the Holy Spirit. (See Galatians 5:22–23.) Neither does it make a person mature. Indeed, the Corinthians were baptized, yet immature and carnal. (See 1 Corinthians 14:22.)

Neither does the baptism of the Holy Spirit supernaturally bring all saints into total agreement on every point of doctrine. Even Peter and Paul disagreed over doctrine and yet were baptized. (See Galatians 2:1–15; Acts 15.)

The baptism of the Holy Spirit does not mean that the receiver of this blessing becomes a mindless person residing in a self-hypnotic state. Rather, the baptism of the Holy Spirit refers to a great and earnest quest for God, which will lead us to the place where God can be found as much in power as we can experience Him in this life.

In consequence, the baptism of the Holy Spirit is used to assist and allow the saint under his or her will to work, not in their own power, but in the power of the Holy Spirit to grow continually in their spiritual life, progress in their sanctification, and continue in their spiritual training into the truth by the Holy Spirit Himself. (See Romans 8:14; John 17:17; 14:26; 16:13.)

If a believer is baptized by the Holy Spirit, the result will also be that he is filled. But, if a believer is filled by the Holy Spirit, it is open to question whether the believer will accept being baptized by the Holy Spirit.

All believers are filled with the Holy Spirit but are not baptized by that same Spirit. (See Romans 8:9–16; 1 Corinthians 3:16, 12:13.) In other words, if one is baptized with the Holy Spirit, then one is both filled and baptized as seen on the Day of Pentecost. On the other hand, if one is filled, then he may or may not be baptized. One who is baptized can have multiple fillings.

The filling mentioned in Acts 2:4 was just one of many that most of those present in the upper room experienced. Why? Many fillings kept coming to them to replenish the Spirit and power they had received. (See Acts 4:8, 31; 13:52.) Therefore, one must continue to live and walk in the Holy Spirit in order to continually be baptized with the Holy Spirit. (See Ephesians 3:16–20; 5:18; Galatians 5:16–26.) If not, the believer will lose the baptism of the Holy Spirit and its benefits.

All believers are baptized into Christ, but not all believers are baptized into the Holy Spirit. (See Romans 6:4; 12:4–5; 1 Corinthians 10:17; 12:13; Galatians 3:3–5, 27; Ephesians 4:5; Colossians 2:12; Isaiah 11:2; 28:9–12; Joel 2:28–29; Matthew 3:11; Luke 3:16–22; John 1:29–42; 2 Timothy 1:7; 2:21; 3:5.)

There are several reasons to experience the baptism of the Holy Spirit:

☦ It imparts to the believer the power for service within the community of saints and within the entire world. (See Acts 1:8.)

☦ It opens the spiritual gifts of the Holy Spirit to the believer. (See 1 Corinthians 12:7–11.)

☦ It causes the believer to embrace the spiritual gifts of the Holy Spirit. (See 1 Corinthians 12:7–11.)

☦ It causes the believer to embrace the vision of the early church and the freshness of their calling. (See 1 Corinthians 12:7–11.)

☦ The Holy Spirit is able to empower and assist the believer in his infirmities and weaknesses. (See Romans 8:26.)

☦ It increases the prayer life of a believer. In other words, it bestows upon the believer an intensified prayer life. (See Romans 8:26; Jude 20.)

☦ It bestows on the believer more love for Christ,

His Word and the lost. (See Acts 4:24–37; 5:29; 1
Corinthians 14:1.)

✝ It gives the believer the power to fight against
Satan, his devices and his temptations. (See
Galatians 5:16; James 4:7.)

✝ It blesses the believer with edification, joy and
blessings. (See 1 Corinthians 14:4.)

✝ It gives rest to the weary. (See Isaiah 28:11–12.)

✝ It bestows on the believer a greater revelation
and vision of both Christ and His Word. (See
John 14:26; 16:13–14.)

✝ It gives the believer the very empowerment and
ability to do greater numbers of works than
Christ did. (See John 14:12.)

✝ It confirms, proves and authenticates the Word
of God. (See Mark 16:20; Hebrews 2:3–4.)

✝ It continues the things that Jesus Himself did
and taught. (See Acts 1:1–2; Matthew 28:20.)

✝ It makes the believer successful in witnessing to
a lost and dying world. (See Acts 1:8.)

✝ It proves and authenticates that people are truly
sent by God, His witnesses, His believers and His
representatives. (See Mark 16:15–20; John 14:12;
Acts 1:8.)

✝ It is a command of Christ. (See Luke 24:49; Acts
1:4–5.)

✝ It bestows on the believer an immersion in the
Holy Spirit, not as previously experienced. (See
Acts 2:1–15.)

✝ It brings forth the belief that the saints must
keep the "old man" crucified. (See Romans 6:6.)

✝ It brings new life to the Scriptures. In other
words, the baptism of the Holy Spirit gives life to
the Scriptures. (See Isaiah 30:18.)

✝ The reality of Satan is opened to the mind, eyes,
spirit and life of the saints. (See Matthew 4:1–11;
John 10:10.)

One can receive the baptism of the Holy Spirit by doing all of the following things—together, not separately:

✝ By being born again. (See John 14:17; Acts 19:2.)

✝ By asking. (See Luke 11:13.)

✝ By surrendering. (See Romans 12:1.)

✝ By being willing to obey the Spirit. (See Acts 5:32.)

✝ By believing in the baptism of the Holy Spirit. (See Galatians 3:2, 14.)

✝ By exercising in faith what one has received. (See Acts 2:4.)

Today the gifts of the Spirit are only given without measure. In this case, the baptism of the Holy Spirit is essential to receiving them in this capacity. Without the baptism of the Holy Spirit, the gifts cannot be manifested in a person's life, even if that person has a filling of the Holy Spirit. These gifts are without measure. They are no longer given by measure.

However, it is very possible for a believer, before he has been baptized in the Holy Spirit, to have been told by God through prophecy what gifts will be manifested in his life as soon as he experiences the baptism. It is even possible for the baptism of the Holy Spirit to be lost by a believer and for him to lose all that he has gained through it. When the baptism of the Holy Spirit is lost so are all the gifts bestowed by God.

It is not possible for a saint of God to lose the baptism of the Holy Spirit and retain the gift of tongues. As long as there is a spark of that baptism within the saint, there will remain the gift of tongues. That is why the baptism of the Holy Spirit must be rekindled from time to time through prayer, fasting, praying for people and studying the Word of God.

The baptism of the Holy Spirit is weakened in a saint's life when he or she becomes lukewarm. Those trained to minister in a prophetic calling may see no spark of the Spirit still in these people, or it would seem that the saint has lost his baptism. Yet a flicker of life may remain that only God can see.

In other instances, a saint of God has become so lukewarm that he not only has lost the baptism but also the gift of tongues. It is very possible in these cases of lukewarmness that counterfeit tongues will emerge. (See 1 Corinthians 12:3; 1 John 4:4; Matthew 7:16–20.) In such an instance, the counterfeit tongues may fool the one who has backslidden.

The fruits of the Holy Spirit are not the baptism of the Holy Spirit. The fruits of the Holy Spirit are for holiness while the baptism of the Holy Spirit is for power.

In Acts 2:28 and Acts 10:45 the baptism of the Holy Spirit is known as a gift. The Greek noun is δωρεά (thōrĕä). On the other hand, the gifts recorded in 1 Corinthians 12–14 are mentioned by Paul as χάρισμα (khärēsmä). The use of different nouns is an indication that the baptism of the Holy Spirit is not one of the gifts mentioned by Paul but rather comes before the gifts.

In addition, the different nouns indicate that the gifts of the Holy Spirit mentioned by Paul are a result of the gift of the Holy Spirit temporarily, permanently, completely and even partially. Hence, the baptism of the Holy Spirit must be exercised so that the gifts can be given by the Holy Spirit to a believer. The position of the gifts of the Holy Spirit in the believer and their exercise depends on the state of the believer and his being under the submission of the Holy Spirit.

The Greek noun δωρεά (thōrĕä) in Acts 2:28 and Acts 10:45 literally means "formal endowment of the Holy Spirit, reception of the Holy Spirit, the giving of the Holy Spirit for power, and receiving the favor and benefit of the Holy Spirit without measure."

The Greek noun χάρισμα (khärēsmä) in 1 Corinthians 12–14 denotes "the manifestations and endowments of the Holy Spirit that enter into the reality of the believer, the church, and the world." They are the manifestations of the merciful and graceful Spirit for the sake of believers. They are also the manifestations of the Holy Spirit in all His graces that He alone bestows.

The Holy Spirit is the only source and agent who baptizes believers into Christ and then into the church. (See 1 Corinthians 12:13; Galatians 3:27; Romans 6:3; Colossians 2:12.) On the other hand, Christ is the only source and agent who baptizes the believer into the Holy Spirit. (See Matthew 3:11; Luke 3:16; John 1:33; Acts 1-2, 5; 11:16; Luke 11:13; John 7:37-39.)

In other words, in Matthew 3:11, Luke 3:16, John 1:33, Acts 1:5 and Acts 11:16, the baptism of the Holy Spirit is mentioned. In these passages, the baptizer of the Holy Spirit is Christ Himself, especially in Matthew 3:11 and Luke 3:16. Christ Himself is the source, cause and means of this baptism. The Holy Spirit Himself is the source, cause and means of the filling.

The baptism into Christ is the one baptism mentioned in Ephesians 4:5 that all people must experience in order to encounter the new birth and be found in the community of saints. In other words, the baptism into Christ is the baptism that all people must have in order to be saved and to be found in the community of saints.

Therefore, the baptism into Christ is a necessity for salvation and is the very baptism that purifies the sinner from all his sins. It makes the sinner a new creation in Christ Jesus and gives that newly saved believer a holy right to partake of water baptism and Spirit baptism. (See John 3:3-5; 2 Corinthians 5:17; Romans 6:1-8; Galatians 3:27; Colossians 1:11-13.)

Please notice that there are different Greek constructions used to write the baptism into Christ and the baptism of the Holy Spirit.[1] Comparing all these constructions together, we can see that the baptism into Christ is not grammatically the same as the baptism of the Holy Spirit. There is no foundation that can be used to grammatically prove that they are. On the contrary, there is clear proof from Greek grammar alone that these baptisms are different.

The initial evidence of the baptism of the Holy Spirit is speaking in tongues. (See Acts 2:1–4; 8:14–18; 10:44–46; 19:7; Isaiah 28:11–12; Joel 2:28–29; Matthew 18:16; Acts 8:18–23; Acts 2:39.) Speaking in tongues cannot be the only evidence, but it is the preliminary evidence. A person cannot experience this baptism without the manifestation of speaking in tongues. However, it is possible that the baptism of the Holy Spirit will be bestowed to a person in a dormant state and only be manifested when the person speaks in tongues. The baptism will not be seen as taking effect, though, until the person speaks in tongues.

Tertullian speaks of tongues as *evidence.*[2] What are tongues evidence of? Speaking in tongues is the preliminary evidence that the person has received the Holy Spirit.

This manifestation of speaking in tongues may be so quiet and stated with so few words that even the person himself may not recognize that he has spoken in tongues. This explains why people have exercised the gifts of the Holy Spirit and yet thought that they had never spoken in tongues. They did, but it was only temporarily.

There are functional degrees within all the gifts of the Spirit. This means that some manifest and function in a certain gift more so than others, while some manifest and function in a certain gift less than others. Even tongues can be spoken more by one person than by other persons, as witnessed by Paul. (See 1 Corinthians 14:18.)

Tongues also may lay dormant for years after they are first manifested at the baptism of the Holy Spirit and only later, due to a desire for that blessing to be restored, become active again in that person's life. Some people may speak just a few words all their lives in the same language while others speak countless words in many types of languages.

In Acts 10:44–46 the gift of the Holy Spirit, which is the baptism of the Holy Spirit, fell on the Gentiles at Cæsarea. Verse 46 reads, "For they heard them speak in tongues."

The "for" is translated from the Greek conjunction γάρ (gär) and is used to represent a causal clause. The causal clause denotes that Peter and the six Jewish believers knew that the Gentiles were truly baptized in the Holy Spirit because the Gentiles spoke in tongues. (See Acts 10:23–11:12.) It was by this reason and evidence that Peter and his contemporaries knew they were baptized.

It was because of this that Peter and the six Jewish believers knew that the Gentiles had received the same Spirit baptism that they also had received approximately eight years before at Pentecost. (See Acts 2:1–4.)

Acts 10:44–46 indicates that the baptism of the Holy Spirit, with the initial evidence of speaking in tongues, can be given to men immediately after their conversion— within seconds—sometime after their conversion. (See Acts 2:1–11; 8:12–23; 9:17–18; 19:1–7.) This baptism can also be given before water baptism or after water baptism. (See Matthew 3:16–17; Acts 2:1–11; 8:4–23; 9:1–7, 17–18.)

Remarkably, the early church held that the baptism of the Holy Spirit, which was also known by them as the reception of the Spirit, was not the baptism into Christ but something following it. In other words, the baptism of the Holy Spirit was separate from being saved.

The great leader Cyprian wrote:

> For if the apostle does not speak falsely when he says, "As many of you as are baptized into Christ, have put on Christ," certainly he who has been baptized among them into Christ has put on Christ. But if he has put on Christ, he might also receive the Holy Ghost, who was sent by Christ, and hands are vainly laid upon him who comes to us for the reception of the Spirit; unless, perhaps, he has not put on the spirit from Christ, so that Christ indeed may be with heretics, but the Holy Spirit may not be with them.[3]

An anonymous bishop of the Christian church in the third century, dealing with rebaptism of heretics, writes:

But they who are not ignorant of the nature of the Holy Spirit, understand that what is said of fire is said of the Spirit Himself. For in the Acts of the Apostles, according to that same promise of our Lord, on the very day of Pentecost, when the Holy Spirit had descended upon the disciples, that they might be baptized in Him, there were seen sitting upon each one tongues as if of fire, that it might be manifest that they were baptized with the Holy Spirit and with fire.[4]

This ancient writer sets forth that the baptism of the Holy Spirit is different from conversion and that the initial evidence of the baptism of the Holy Spirit is speaking in tongues. This ancient writer, who is always overlooked by those who demand that this baptism is the same thing as conversion, taught that:

✝ Spiritual baptism—baptism of the Holy Spirit—is separated from evangelical baptism—water baptism and baptism of repentance or what is known as the baptism into Christ.

✝ Spiritual baptism is proved from Matthew 3:11, Acts 1:4–5, 11:5–7, 15:7–8.

✝ Believe in Christ and receive spiritual baptism afterward.

✝ Spiritual baptism is an additional or subsequent baptism from conversion.

✝ The baptism of the Holy Spirit is given to everyone who believes, as with the Samaritans and after Philip's baptism.

✝ Those who believe in Christ need to be baptized with the Spirit.

✝ Spiritual baptism can be given before water baptism, as witnessed from Acts 10:44–48 and Acts 15:9.

✝ Speaking in tongues accompanies spiritual baptism.

✝ The disciples were baptized in water, but later

were baptized with the Spirit.

✞ Spiritual baptism is known as the baptism of the Holy Spirit.

✞ The baptism of the Holy Spirit is connected to the prophecy of Joel. (See Acts 2:17–18.)

✞ The baptism of the Holy Spirit either goes before or follows water baptism.[5]

OVERVIEW OF CHAPTER FOUR

The Filling and the Baptisms

1. From the Greek text itself, the baptism of the Holy Spirit is not seen to be the same as the filling of the Holy Spirit, nor the baptism into Christ.

2. The Greek text shows that there are differences among all three experiences.

3. The filling of the Holy Spirit, mentioned in Acts 2:4, cannot be seen as the promise of the Comforter to baptize believers with the Holy Spirit, but it must be seen as the result of such baptism.

4. Notice that not all experienced the baptism of the Holy Spirit and the filling of the Holy Spirit at Pentecost.

5. The filling of the Holy Spirit is receiving the Holy Spirit in measure, while the baptism of the Holy Spirit is receiving the Holy Spirit in His fullness.

6. The baptism of the Holy Spirit is not the fruits of the Holy Spirit.

7. The baptism of the Holy Spirit does not deal with holiness.

8. The baptism of the Holy Spirit does not make every saint perfect or cause them to be in total conformity with one another.

9. The baptism of the Holy Spirit does not make a saint mindless or create a self-hypnotic state.

10. The baptism of the Holy Spirit is a great and earnest quest for God.

11. The baptism of the Holy Spirit empowers, assists and allows the saint under His will to work in the power of the Holy Spirit.

12. If a saint is baptized by the Holy Spirit, he will be filled. But if one is filled, he won't necessarily be baptized.

13. All believers are filled, but not all believers are baptized. (See Romans 8:9–16; 1 Corinthians 3:16; 12:13.)

14. All saints are baptized into Christ, but not all are baptized into the Holy Spirit.

15. There are several reasons for experiencing the baptism of the Holy Spirit:

    ✞ It imparts to the believer the power for service within the community of saints and within the entire world. (See Acts 1:8.)

    ✞ It opens to the believer the spiritual gifts of the Holy Spirit. (See 1 Corinthians 12:7–11.)

    ✞ It causes the believer to embrace the spiritual gifts of the Holy Spirit. (See 1 Corinthians 12:7–11.)

    ✞ It causes the believer to embrace the vision of the early church and the freshness of his calling. (See 1 Corinthians 12:7–11.)

    ✞ The Holy Spirit is able to empower, assist and help the believer in his infirmities and weaknesses. (See Romans 8:26.)

    ✞ It increases the prayer life of a believer by bestowing on the believer an intensified prayer life. (See Romans 8:26; Jude 20.)

    ✞ It bestows on the believer more love for Christ,

His Word and the lost. (See Acts 4:24–37; 5:29; 1 Corinthians 14:1.)

✝ It gives the believer the power to fight against Satan, his devices and his temptations. (See Galatians 5:16; James 4:7.)

✝ It blesses the believer with edification, joy and blessings. (See 1 Corinthians 14:4.)

✝ It gives rest to the weary. (See Isaiah 28:11–12.)

✝ It bestows on the believer a greater revelation and vision of both Christ and His Word. (See John 14:26; 16:13–14.)

✝ It gives the believer the very empowerment and ability to do more works than Christ did. (See John 14:12.)

✝ It confirms, proves and authenticates the Word of God. (See Mark 16:20; Hebrews 2:3–4.)

✝ It continues the things that Jesus Himself did and taught. (See Acts 1:1–2; Matthew 28:20.)

✝ It makes the believer successful in witnessing to a lost and dying world. (See Acts 1:8.)

✝ It proves and authenticates that people are truly sent by God, that they are His witnesses, His believers and His representatives. (See Mark 16:15–20; John 14:12; Acts 1:8.)

✝ It is a command of Christ. (See Luke 24:49; Acts 1:4–5.)

✝ It bestows upon the believer an immersion into the Holy Spirit not previously experienced. (See Acts 2:1–15.)

✝ It brings forth the belief that the saints must keep the "old man" crucified. (See Romans 6:6.)

✝ It gives life to the Scriptures. (See Isaiah 30:18.)

✝ The reality of Satan is opened to the mind, eyes, spirit and life of the saints. (See Matthew 4:1–11; John 10:10.)

16. One can receive the baptism of the Holy Spirit by doing all of the following things together:

✝ By being born again. (See John 14:17; Acts 19:2.)

✝ By asking. (See Luke 11:13.)

✝ By surrendering. (See Romans 12:1.)

✝ By being willing to obey the Spirit. (See Acts 5:32.)

✝ By believing in the baptism of the Holy Spirit. (See Galatians 3:2; 3:14.)

✝ By exercising in faith what one has received. (See Acts 2:4.)

17. Today, the gifts of the Spirit are given only without measure.

18. The baptism of the Holy Spirit is known as a "gift" in Acts 2:28 and Acts 10:45.

19. The Holy Spirit is seen as the only source and agent who baptizes believers into Christ and then into the church. (See 1 Corinthians 12:13; Galatians 3:27; Romans 6:3; Colossians 2:12.)

20. The baptism into Christ is the one baptism mentioned in Ephesians 4:5.

21. The initial evidence of the baptism of the Holy Spirit is speaking in tongues.

22. The early church held that the baptism of the Holy Spirit was not the baptism into Christ. It would follow the baptism into Christ.

Chapter Five

First Corinthians on Tongues

First Corinthians 12–14 deals with spiritual gifts, their characteristics, purpose, function and restrictions. Certain passages will be explained in detail and will be numbered and placed in two separate sections—one dealing with 1 Corinthians 12–13; the other dealing only with 1 Corinthians 14. Before these passages are dealt with separately, we must first look at some general facts about 1 Corinthians.

BACKGROUND TO FIRST CORINTHIANS

The explanation of 1 Corinthians 14 involves general facts mentioned by Paul in this chapter and the very fact that the restrictions of 1 Corinthians 14 are not seen by the early church and by Greek grammar as universal in effect but only restricted and limited. In consequence, the restrictions of 1 Corinthians 14 can no longer be used as a battering ram against speaking in tongues.

What were these restrictions? These restrictions will be worded as they commonly are by those who rebuke the gift of tongues and its use:

✝ Tongues are not to be spoken in a congregation without being interpreted. (See 1 Corinthians 14:27–28a.)

✝ Tongues are not to be spoken when it is time to preach the gospel of Christ. (See 1 Corinthians 14:6–14, 19, 23–25.)

✦ Tongues are not to be spoken when invited to give thanksgiving or grace. (See 1 Corinthians 14:16–17.)

✦ Tongues are not to be spoken in a congregation when the unlearned and unbelievers are present. (See 1 Corinthians 14:23–25.)

✦ Tongues are not to be spoken after two or three messages have been given and interpreted. (See 1 Corinthians 14:27–28a.)

✦ Tongues are not to be spoken by women in the church. (See 1 Corinthians 14:34–35.)

In dealing with Paul's first epistle to the Corinthian church, one must from the onset bear in mind several general facts:

✦ Paul was answering a letter the Corinthians had written to him.

✦ Paul's answer was directed toward the whole body of the Corinthian church.

✦ Paul was teaching the Corinthians in the first six chapters of the book. From chapter seven to the end of 1 Corinthians, Paul was answering specific things they had written to him about. (See 1 Corinthians 7:10, 18, 25; 8:1; 9:1; 10:1–6; 11:1.)

✦ In this dialogue between Paul and the Corinthians, some answers came from God and others came from Paul's own judgment. For example, 1 Corinthians 11:3–15 is Paul's judgment. Verse 16 counteracts that judgment if confusion occurs about verses 3–15.

The Gift of Tongues in Corinthians

The phenomenon of speaking in tongues mentioned by Paul in 1 Corinthians 12–14 is the same thing that occurred on the Day of Pentecost. It is the functioning of the same gift and comes from the same source. The same source is seen to be the Holy Spirit. This phenomenon is an endowment of the Holy Spirit. (See Acts 2:4.)

The peculiar phenomenon of speaking in tongues in

1 Corinthians 12–14 is linked absolutely to the phenomenon mentioned in Mark 16:17 and in Acts 2:4.

Within 1 Corinthians 12–14 Paul gives his experience with the gift of tongues, describes its characteristics, its function and in a limited sense its purpose. The experience of Paul with the gift of tongues is the same that other Christians have experienced and do experience. The characteristics and function of the gift of tongues described by Paul are universal in effect. The purpose of the gift of tongues stated by Paul is one-sided. He does not give the full significance of the gift of tongues. It is his intention to limit its significance and purpose at Corinth.

Outside of Corinth Paul recognizes the full significance of the gift of tongues and its full significance as a sign, but he desires to restrain its significance at Corinth due to the Corinthians' carnality and immaturity. After carnality and immaturity have disappeared, the full significance can again be experienced at Corinth. Because Paul limits the purpose of the gift of tongues at Corinth, the restrictions are also limited by Paul only at Corinth, which will be proved.

According to Paul, speaking in tongues is a gift that is used either to be interpreted by men or not to be interpreted by anyone but God. (See 1 Corinthians 14:2.) Tongues can be used as ministering tongues, which must be interpreted, or as praying tongues, which are not to be interpreted by anyone except God. Tongues are called praying tongues when they are formed into prayers and are not to be used for interpretation.

Tongues, whether for ministry or prayer, can be used also for praise, thanksgiving, blessing or even singing. (See 1 Corinthians 14:2, 14–15; Acts 2:11–15; 10:46.) Both ministering tongues and praying tongues can be the same tongue, only used differently. In this case, the tongue at one time would be interpreted by men, and at another time it would be interpreted by God.

In consequence, tongues are Holy Spirit-affected

speech from man to God. Tongues are only spoken from man to man for interpretation. (See 1 Corinthians 14:2, 14–15, 28b.)

In Corinth, speaking in tongues was desired above all other gifts. The other gifts were almost denied and abandoned. There is enough in Paul's writing to show that the Corinthian peculiarities were disgraceful accretions and abuses. They made tongues a source of apostasy in the church. They did this by exalting the gift of tongues above all other gifts and by restricting the direction of the Holy Spirit in the gift of tongues and setting up their own direction.

When the Holy Spirit directs the gift of tongues within a particular church, there is no need for restrictions. The Corinthians grieved the Holy Spirit in attempting to direct this gift themselves, which they failed to do. In effect, they were resisting the Holy Spirit.

If this is the case, why did the Holy Spirit still allow the gift of tongues to be present in the Corinthian church? The benefits of speaking in tongues will always overcome the abuses and shortcomings brought forth by men. Indeed, speaking in tongues is the preliminary evidence of the baptism of the Holy Spirit.

Speaking in tongues does not bring abuse, carnality and immaturity. On the contrary, speaking in tongues in its true essence is a call back to the Word of God. The Word of God is where maturity is found and carnality is destroyed.

The Corinthian saints had another main problem. They had over-realized eschatology. They placed themselves in the millennial reign of Christ when the millennial kingdom had not (and has not yet) come forth. (See 1 Corinthians 4:8–21.) They taught an ancient form of "kingdom now" theology, believing that they were already reigning as kings, when Paul himself was reigning as a servant. (See Romans 1:1; Titus 1:1.)

Beyond this, the Corinthian church was a divided church with many factions about many things. (See 1 Corinthians

1:12; 7–12.) Utter confusion reigned in the Corinthian church because of their carnality and immaturity, not because of the gifts found there or the moving of the Holy Spirit. It was the result of the vessels, not the gifts. The gifts at present always work in imperfect vessels.

Other problems within the Corinthian church included:

✝ A love existed for so-called philosophy and eloquence. (See 1 Corinthians 1:17.)

✝ Disgraceful immorality was tolerated among the Corinthian church. (See 1 Corinthians 5.)

✝ Lawsuits were carried out. (See 1 Corinthians 6.)

✝ There was immoral indulgence. (See 1 Corinthians 6:9–20.)

✝ The Lord's supper had become perverted. (See 1 Corinthians 11:20–34.)

✝ There was the idea that the church was a social hall and not a place to worship and praise God. (See 1 Corinthians 11:20–24.)

In the experience of Acts 2, the majority of all manifestations of tongues were for the purpose of ministry. As a result, the majority of these manifestations were to be interpreted—and were—by the onlookers. (See Acts 2:1–15.) But this means of interpretation did not come from the gift of interpretation of tongues. It came through the natural ability of the onlookers to know their own language.

To Paul, the main value of the gift of tongues was for the individual rather than for the Christian community, a church meeting or a congregation as a whole. (See 1 Corinthians 14:2, 4, 28b.) Yet Paul stresses in his restrictions the opposite, for the sake of the Corinthians.

To Paul there were various kinds of tongues, more than just human. (See 1 Corinthians 12:10, 28; 13:1.) The messages that are being spoken by the Holy Spirit through the gift of tongues can only become intelligible and understandable for the whole congregation and all other creatures when either the speaker or another saint gives an interpretation. (See 1 Corinthians 14:5; 12:10, 30.)

Praying tongues are never to become intelligible and understandable for any creature of God. Only God comprehends and understands what is being spoken. Ministering tongues are those that become intelligible through the gift of interpretation of tongues. They become understandable for the whole congregation, for just the speaker or for the speaker and one or more other people.

When one is under this Holy Spirit-inspired utterance, the understanding is overwhelmed and suppressed so that these words are mysteries to the speaker and even to the hearers unless interpretation can be given. (See 1 Corinthians 14:14.)

NO RESTRICTIONS ON TONGUES IN EFFECT

The restrictions laid on the gift of tongues by Paul in 1 Corinthians 14, namely verses 6–14, 16–17, 19, 23–25, 27–28a and 34–35, can no longer be seen as universal but limited in effect and only at Corinth, from the ensuing arguments:

1. It must be stated that the practice of speaking in tongues in Acts 10:44–46; 19:6; 11:15 has no restrictions on it. In these passages, according to Greek thought, there is freedom in the function of the gift of tongues as the Holy Spirit gives utterance, with no limitation or restriction at all.

Unquestionably, all spoke together in Acts 10:44–46 and 19:6. The message here is that before Paul's proclamation in 1 Corinthians 14:1–40, which stressed restrictions, no such restrictions were given by any other apostle of God. This is important. Why? It limits Paul's restrictions to just Corinth and not to other places where the practice of speaking in tongues also manifested itself—Ephesus (Acts 19:6), Jerusalem (Acts 2), Thessalonica (1 Thess. 5:19), Rome (Rom. 8:26) or Cæsarea (Acts 10:44–46).

Paul would have been the most hypocritical person you could have met if he had meant the restrictions on the gift of tongues were universal in effect. Did not Paul lay hands

on believers and they spoke in tongues at Ephesus? (See
Acts 19:6.) Notice that the believers spoke in tongues
without any restrictions.

In A.D. 54 no restrictions were placed on the gift of
tongues at Ephesus. In A.D. 57 restrictions were placed on
this gift at Corinth.

The only fact that can save Paul from hypocrisy is that
he placed these restrictions only on the Corinthian church
and no other. Even Paul himself did not follow these
restrictions at Ephesus, Thessalonica and at Rome.

Notice that Paul had four missionary journeys:

- ✞ The first missionary journey is recorded in Acts
  13:1 to Acts 14:28 and took place from A.D. 45–47.

- ✞ The second missionary journey is recorded in
  Acts 15:36 to Acts 18:22 and took place from A.D.
  50–54.

- ✞ The third missionary journey is recorded in Acts
  18:23 to Acts 21:17 and took place from A.D.
  54–58.

- ✞ The fourth and last missionary journey is
  recorded in Acts 21:17 to Acts 28:31 and took
  place from A.D. 58–67.

From these journeys, one should pay close attention to
the fact that no restrictions were instituted on the gift of
tongues in the first, second, fourth and beginning of the
third missionary journey. They were, however, instituted
in the latter part of the third missionary journey.

Notice that in the second missionary journey, Paul did
not form or place restrictions on the gift of tongues at
Corinth. (See Acts 18:1–22.) No restrictions were laid on
the gift of tongues throughout all these journeys at any
place except Corinth—not in Syria, Cilicia, Derbe, Lystra,
Phrygia, Galatia, Troas, Philippi, Amphipolis, Apollonia,
Thessalonica, Berea, Athens, Cenchrea, Ephesus,
Caesarea, Jerusalem or other places.

According to apostolic authority, these restrictions
were—in the early church before the fourth century—

directed only at the Corinthian church. There is no hint by any father of the church before the fourth century that these restrictions were applied to other particular churches. Neither can this hint be found by Paul through Greek grammar. The restrictions are absolutely limited to the Corinthian church.

Even if a particular church is seen as immature and carnal, there is no apostolic authority, apostolic father or father before the fourth century who links these restrictions to it. In essence, to link these restrictions to any church other than the Corinthian church is following a course of interpretation that was unknown to the early church.

It does seem, for the sake of holiness and necessity, that a carnal and immature church could well take these restrictions and reenact them. However, this would be contrary to the nature and purpose of these restrictions. Every church that uses these restrictions is in essence suggesting that they are carnal and immature.

2. Carnality and immaturity of the Corinthian saints are the only reasons that restrictions were laid on the gift of tongues. (See 1 Corinthians 14:22.) Where there is no carnality and immaturity within a church, and where the Holy Spirit directs the gifts, no restrictions are needed. No restrictions were found in the other church communities.

3. Grammatically, Paul sets forth the idea that the restrictions laid on the gift of tongues are not to be seen as universal and perpetual. He sees them as only temporary for the Corinthian church. Paul says that the restrictions are according to the commandment of the Lord. (See 1 Corinthians 14:37.) Yet, this commandment, according to Greek grammar, was given for the Corinthian church as temporary measure until they could function in the gifts without these strict rules.

Proof that the restrictions are temporary and conditional is found by using the *subjunctive, imperative* and *optative* moods within Paul's dialogue with the Corinthians. Also, notice that Paul is speaking directly to the Corinthians and not to the other Christian communities about the gifts of the Holy Spirit.

Out of 40 verses in 1 Corinthians 14, the *subjunctive mood* appears 25 times. (See 1 Corinthians 14:1, 5–9, 12–14, 16, 19, 23–24, 26, 28, 30–31.)

The *imperative mood* appears 21 times. (See 1 Corinthians 14:1, 12–13, 20, 26–27, 29–30, 34–35, 37, 39–40.)

The *optative mood* appears once. (See 1 Corinthians 14:10.) The use of these moods overpowers the thought of the indicative mood.

Paul's use of these moods devastates the essential element of the argument that only the gift of tongues should be manifested according to regulations and order referred to by Paul in 1 Corinthians 14. The use of these other moods literally means that these restrictions are not to be taken as absolute, universal and perpetual, but only temporary, conditional and limited in effect.

The application of the *subjunctive mood* in 1 Corinthians 14, besides that of the *imperative* and *optative* moods, brings into the equation the thought of uncertainty, plausibility, the will of the Holy Spirit and the will of the believer. It recognizes that the restrictions were placed on the Corinthian church for the sake of holiness and necessity so that the Corinthian church would not enter into a state of fanaticism and would be pulled out of carnality and immaturity. There is no proof here that these restrictions were to be placed on the manifestations of the Holy Spirit throughout all other Christian communities.

The presence of uncertainty and plausibility within 1 Corinthians 14 illustrates the temporary, conditional and limited nature of these restrictions. The presence of these grammatical moods signifies that the restrictions were limited only to the Corinthian church and that these restrictions would be temporary at Corinth if their carnality and immaturity disappeared.

The presence of the *subjunctive, imperative,* and *optative*

moods in 1 Corinthians 14 does affect the characteristics
and function of the gift of tongues, but not in the same
manner as they affect the restrictions. These moods limit
the restrictions of the gift of tongues to just the Corinthian
church. These moods do not limit the characteristics and
functions of the gift of tongues, mentioned by Paul just to
Corinth.

The characteristics and function of the gift of tongues
are influenced in three main ways by the moods:

> ✝ The first result is that the gift of tongues and the
> gift of prophecy are seen as temporary; that is,
> the characteristics and the function of the gift of
> tongues will cease. (See 1 Corinthians 13:8–10.)

> ✝ The second result is that manifestation of the
> characteristics and functions of this gift within a
> particular church may vary under the direction
> of the Holy Spirit. While all the characteristics
> and functions of this gift are the same
> throughout all Christian communities, there is a
> possibility that not all characteristics and func-
> tions of this gift will work in a particular church
> the same way or in the same method as others.
> Also, it is plausible that some characteristics and
> functions will be silent in one church and loud
> and present in another.

> ✝ The third result is that every manifestation of
> the characteristics and functions of this gift may
> be conditional, limited in one way or another,
> and may temporarily come and go within a par-
> ticular church.

> 4. Paul, by invoking these restrictions, placed a stran-
> glehold on the gift of tongues at Corinth, due to
> their carnality and immaturity. He set forth such
> strict rules and standards for the Corinthians that
> we wonder whether the gift of tongues could have
> survived as a manifestation of the Holy Spirit at
> Corinth if they followed his strict regulations.

Paul may be seen by some here as a tyrant or even as
one who restricts the liberty of Christians. However, the

restrictions were necessary in this instance. It was a way for the Holy Spirit to begin again in the lives of the Corinthians, as it pertained to the gifts. It was a way for fanaticism to be kept out of the Corinthian church; it was also a way for the gift of prophecy and other gifts to be placed in their honorable position within the Corinthian church and not abandoned or denied any longer.

The grammatical moods cannot be used to show that the restrictions themselves were not strict or severe. On the contrary, the moods, other than the indicative mood, do not limit the severest of the restrictions but only their effects on Corinth and no other Christian community.

5. No apostolic father who lived in the first and second centuries supported the continuation of the restrictions on the gift of tongues.

6. No apostolic father mentions the need for such restrictions any longer.

7. The apostolic father Clement wrote nothing about the gift of tongues being restricted. In his epistle to the Corinthians, written in A.D. 95 or 96, there is no hint of any type of continued restrictions being placed on the gift of tongues at Corinth, as mentioned by Paul in A.D. 57. Clement does mention the gifts of the Holy Spirit, yet no restrictions are given.[1]

The old troubles appeared to have passed away from the Corinthian church. There was no more over-realized eschatology being taught, neither were tongues seen any longer as a source of apostasy in the church, nor was immaturity a problem.

The new problem in the Corinthian church was one of sedition against the leaders of the Corinthian church. Some had risen up against the duly commissioned leaders of their church and had ejected them from office. The division and sedition were not because of doctrine, but were due to personal and political conflicts.

8. No part of 1 Corinthians 14 is quoted by the apostolic fathers. If the restrictions were still in effect, one of these men would have mentioned it.

9. Ignatius wrote to the Philippians:

> And there is also one Paraclete. For "there is also," saith [the Scripture], "one Spirit," since "we have been called in one hope of our calling." And again, "We have drunk of one Spirit," with which follows. And it is manifest that all these gifts [possessed by believers] "worketh one and the self-same Spirit.[2]

The fact that Ignatius mentions the gifts without any type of restriction indicates that the restrictions laid on the gift of tongues had no place at Philippi.

10. In the writings of Justin Martyr, there is no mention of restrictions being placed on the gifts of the Holy Spirit, whether tongues or prophecy.

11. Irenæus does mention the gift of tongues three separate times, but no restrictions are found. Irenæus writes in one particular passage:

> For this reason does the apostle declare, "We speak wisdom among them that are perfect," terming those persons "perfect" who have received the Spirit of God, and who through the Spirit of God do speak in all languages, *as he used Himself also to speak.* In like manner we do also hear many brethren in the church, who possess prophetic gifts, and who through the Spirit speak all kinds of languages, and bring to light for the general benefit the hidden things of men, and declare the mysteries of God, whom also the apostle terms "spiritual," they being spiritual because they partake of the Spirit, and not because their flesh has been stripped off and taken away, and because they have become purely spiritual.[3]

12. Clement of Alexandria mentions 1 Corinthians 12:7–11, 4:20 and 14:6–13, but he alludes to no restrictions on any gift, whether tongues or even prophecies. First Corinthians 14:6–13 is used by Clement not as a restriction but to show that barbarian philosophy is unintelligible and not to be followed in the search for truth. First Corinthians 14:9–13 is used by Clement out of context and is thought to make a point against barbarianism.

13. Lactantius, Hippolytus, Origen, Dionysius of Alexandria, Gregory Thaumaturgus and Julius Africanus saw no restrictions on the gift of tongues. No restrictions are ever mentioned by these writers.

14. In the *Didache,* which was completed no later than A.D. 120, there is no mention of restrictions still in effect on the gift of tongues.[4] In chapter 11 there is a reference about prophets speaking in the Spirit, which is taken as speaking in tongues, and no concern is seen for how to regulate or restrict this phenomenon.

15. Novatian taught that the gift of tongues is directed by the Holy Spirit alone, not by restrictions:

This is He who places prophets in the church, instructs teachers, directs tongues, gives powers and healings, does wonderful works, offers discrimination of spirits, affords powers of government, suggests counsels, and orders and arranges whatever other gifts there are.[5]

16. Both Irenæus and Tertullian categorically state that Jesus Christ spoke in tongues without any restrictions needed.[6]

17. Tertullian saw no restriction on the gift of tongues or the gift of prophecy. In 1 Corinthians 14, he quoted such verses as 15, 20–21, 25–26, 32 and 34–35, but never does he infer the continuation of the restrictions.

Tertullian is the first man to move to the extreme on the issue of women in the church. He takes 1 Corinthians 14:34–35 out of the context used by Paul to limit the roles of women in the church. To him, 1 Corinthians 14:34–35 is not a restriction on the gift of tongues and on how women were using this gift in the Corinthian church but a restriction on all Christian women everywhere. Tertullian cannot be the first father to reassert the restrictions again on the gift of tongues. To Tertullian, 1 Corinthians 14:34–35 has nothing to do with the gift of tongues, but everything to do with Christian women keeping silent in a service. Before Tertullian this view was not accepted.

18. Cyprian quotes 1 Corinthians 14:29–30 but does not use this to indicate that prophets should be regulated and restricted. He sees this passage not as a restriction but as a custom. He used it in his text to describe submission among the saints. He, like Tertullian, uses 1 Corinthians 14:34–35 as a battering ram against women having any role in the church.

19. The first father who reasserts the restrictions on either tongues or prophecies was Victorius, who was a leader of the church in the fourth century. He quotes 1 Corinthians 14:29 and sets forth what Paul wrote to the Corinthian church as the universal rule for all prophets, not just for those at Corinth who were immature. It was in the fourth century that some leaders of the church re-established these restrictions to try to destroy the flame of the prophetic ministry. But this plan did not succeed. Thank God, the prophetic ministry continues from century to century by the grace of God.

In essence, the restrictions placed on the gift of tongues by Paul are seen to have disappeared at the Corinthian church soon after they had been enacted. They never concerned the church at large.

OVERVIEW OF CHAPTER FIVE

Background to 1 Corinthians

1. Bear in mind the following things about 1 Corinthians before studying it:

   ✞ Paul was answering a letter that the Corinthians had written to him.

   ✞ Paul's answer was directed toward the entire body of the Corinthian church.

   ✞ Paul was teaching the Corinthians in the first six chapters of the book. From chapter seven to the end of 1 Corinthians, Paul was answering the specific issues they had written to him about. (See 1 Corinthians 7:10, 18, 25; 8:1; 9:1; 10:1–6; 11:1.)

✝ The answers written in his letter were of two types: Paul attributed some answers as coming from God; others he attributed to his own judgment.

The Gift of Tongues in the Corinthian Church

1. The speaking in tongues mentioned by Paul in Corinthians is the same thing that occurred on the Day of Pentecost.

   ✝ It is the functioning of the same gift and comes from the same source.

   ✝ This source was the Holy Spirit.

2. In Paul's discussion on tongues, he gives his experience with this gift, describes its characteristics, its function and, in a limited sense, its purpose.

3. The purpose of the gift of tongues stated by Paul is one-sided.

4. Paul understands the full significance of the gift of tongues, but he does not focus on it for very good reasons.

   ✝ To Paul, speaking in tongues is a gift used either to be interpreted by men or not to be interpreted by anyone but God. (See 1 Corinthians 14:2.)

   ✝ Tongues are seen as Holy Spirit-affected speaking—not to men, unless for interpretation, but to God. (See 1 Corinthians 14:2, 14–15, 28b.)

5. Within the Corinthian church the gift of tongues was desired above all other gifts.

6. The Corinthians grieved the Holy Spirit by trying to control this gift.

7. There are great benefits from speaking in tongues. These benefits will always overcome the abuses.

8. Speaking in tongues does not bring about spiritual maturity.

9. Speaking in tongues in its true essence is a call back to the Word of God.

10. Problems within the Corinthian church went beyond their abusing the gift of tongues. In addition:

    ✟ They taught an ancient form of "kingdom now" theology. (See 1 Corinthians 4:8–21.)

    ✟ They were a divided church with many factions.

    ✟ They had problems with carnality and immaturity.

    ✟ They had a love for so-called philosophy and eloquence. (See 1 Corinthians 1:17.)

    ✟ They tolerated disgraceful immorality. (See 1 Corinthians 5.)

    ✟ They carried out lawsuits. (See 1 Corinthians 6.)

    ✟ They indulged in immoral behavior. (See 1 Corinthians 6:9–20.)

    ✟ They had perverted the Lord's supper. (See 1 Corinthians 11:20–34.)

    ✟ They embraced the idea that the church was a social hall and not a place to worship and praise God. (See 1 Corinthians 11:20–24.)

11. To Paul, the main value of the gift of tongues was for the individual.

12. Paul witnessed various types of tongues spoken through the gift of tongues, not just human tongues.

No Restrictions on Tongues in Effect Today

1. The restrictions laid upon the gift of tongues by Paul are no longer in effect for the saints of God.

2. Paul placed restrictions on the gift of tongues only for the Corinthian church.

3. There is no apostolic authority that supports the idea that these restrictions were for any Christian body, except the Corinthian church.

4. There is no hint by any father of the church before the fourth century that these restrictions were designated for other churches.

5. The reasons for restrictions being placed on the gift of tongues were carnality and immaturity in the Corinthian church. (See 1 Corinthians 14:22.)

6. Greek grammar demands that the restrictions on the gift of tongues not be viewed as universal and eternal.

7. Greek grammar demands that the restrictions were for the Corinthian church alone.

8. The restrictions Paul placed on the gift of tongues for the Corinthians were:

   ✟ Tongues were not to be spoken in a congregation without being interpreted. (See 1 Corinthians 14:27–28a.)

   ✟ Tongues were not to be spoken when it was time to preach the gospel of Jesus Christ. (See 1 Corinthians 14:6–14, 19, 23–25.)

   ✟ Tongues were not to be spoken for an invitation to give thanksgiving or grace. (See 1 Corinthians 14:16–17.)

   ✟ Tongues were not to be spoken in a congregation when unbelievers or those unlearned in the faith were present. (See 1 Corinthians 14:23–25.)

   ✟ Tongues were not to be spoken after two or three messages had been given and interpreted. (See 1 Corinthians 14:27–28a.)

   ✟ Tongues were not to be spoken by women in the church. (See 1 Corinthians 14:34–35.)

9. Paul is not a tyrant about the gift of tongues.

10. There was no stranglehold placed on the gift of tongues in any other Christian community.

11. No apostolic father who lived in the first and second centuries supported a continuation of the restrictions on the gift of tongues.

12. No part of 1 Corinthians 14 is quoted by the apostolic fathers.

Chapter Six

First Corinthians 12–13 on Tongues

W hen studying the issue of the gift of tongues, many overlook 1 Corinthians 12. However, a full understanding of the gift of tongues cannot be obtained when 1 Corinthians 12 is not grasped. Why? In 1 Corinthians 12, Paul lays out the organization of the gifts and the types of gifts. In addition, Paul recognizes the position each person in the Godhead performs in relation to the gifts. The spiritual gifts and their manifestations are by the Holy Spirit; the administration of the spiritual gifts is by Jesus Christ; the operation of the spiritual gifts is by God the Father.

FIRST CORINTHIANS 12

Generally speaking, 1 Corinthians 12:7 can be used to argue against any who say that the gifts of the Holy Spirit can be used privately for an individual instead of for the entire Christian community, or in a church meeting for an individual. As a result, it is generally seen as firm proof that the gifts are used only for the church as a whole and cannot be used by the Holy Spirit for one individual.

It is also denied that the Holy Spirit can use one gift through a person to give them a message or do something for them. What nonsense! Literally, the text from the Greek reads, "But to each one is given the manifestation of the Spirit to be useful [for profit, for advantage, be profitable]." This translation is no different from the others that are generally given.

However, notice that the Greek participle συμφέρον (sēmfĕrōn) with the article is used to express both individual profit and collective profit. Why? The gifts can be used for the profit of the whole Christian community, a particular church or even an individual. The participle can be translated, "for the common good," if one understands that the common good is for both the individual and for the Christian community.

What good are the gifts if they are limited to the collective good instead of to one person? Christ Himself and all those who were endowed with the gifts of the Holy Spirit in the early church refute this idea. The gifts through these people were used to help individuals and occasionally they were used for the collective good.

In 1 Corinthians 12: 8–10 the number and kind of gifts are given. The interesting point in the Greek text is that the Greek adjectives ἄλλος (älōs) and ἕτερος (ĕtĕrōs) and the Greek conjunction δέ (thĕ) are used together. The Greek adjective ἄλλος (älōs) is used six times, the Greek adjective ἕτερος (ĕtĕrōs) two times and the Greek conjunction δέ (thĕ) seven times. What does all this mean?

First, the application of these three words is placed in verses 8–10 for defining the classification of gifts. In other words, these words written by Paul were used to define how the gifts are classified. To Paul, there are three classes of gifts:

- ♰ The first class is limited only to the gifts that have reference to intellectual power: the word of wisdom, the word of knowledge.

- ♰ The second class is limited only to the gifts that have reference to an exalted faith: the gift of faith, the gift of healing, the gift of working of miracles, the gift of prophecy, the discernment of spirits.

- ♰ The last class is limited only to those gifts having reference to tongues: the gift of tongues, the gift of interpretation of tongues.

The Greek adjective ἄλλος (älōs) in verses 8–10 is used to distinguish kinds within classes while the Greek adjective ἕτερος (ĕtĕrōs) in verses 8–10 is used to distinguish not kinds but classes.

The combining of the Greek adjectives ἄλλος (älōs) and ἕτερος (ĕtĕrōs) together is very surprising. For what Paul is expressing here is very remarkable. Though Paul states categorically that a person can truly be endowed with all the gifts of the Spirit at the same time, as witnessed in the life of Jesus and in his own life, he believes that the endowment of the gifts of the Holy Spirit usually does not concern all the gifts at one time. This is seen from these Greek adjectives. (See Matthew 3:13–16; 8:23–27; John 1:16, 34; Acts 3:9–11; 9:17; 10:28; 13:7–13; 14:3–10; 15:12; 19:1–7; Luke 2:40–42; Romans 1:11; Ephesians 1:8–19; Galatians 2:20; 1 Corinthians 1:10–12; 14:6.)

Paul understands that the Holy Spirit frequently gives out one gift at a time within a classified group. When an individual has been endowed with all members of a classified group, then the Holy Spirit—if the individual is worthy and willing—will endow him with one gift at a time within another classified group.

According to Paul, the Holy Spirit usually moves very slowly in endowing believers with these gifts. This is due largely to the Holy Spirit's allowing the believer to develop in his walk with Christ. As the believer grows, the Holy Spirit will increasingly endow that believer with the supernatural gifts.

The gift of tongues in 1 Corinthians 12:10 and 1 Corinthians 12:28 is commonly translated as "kinds of tongues." The Greek noun γένος (yĕnōs) denotes here that the gift of tongues is endowed with families, classes, kinds, races, species and modes. Therefore, Paul indicates the diversity in the tongues.

From this noun Paul shows that there is no limit to the tongues that are found to express the gift of tongues as long as they are intelligible and genuine languages.

Furthermore, Paul incorporates into his view the very notion that every genuine manifestation of speaking in tongues that has appeared in the dispensation of grace, and continues, comes from this gift. Genuine speaking in tongues flows from this gift. There cannot be any genuine speaking in tongues that does not flow from this gift of the Holy Spirit. There are not two rivers, but one river of this genuine phenomenon.

The Greek noun γένος (yĕnōs) places the tongues as an absolute diversity. Because of this, tongues are seen as more than just human or even angelic. Paul sets forth that all types of languages can be employed by the Holy Spirit in the gift of tongues.

This means that to Paul there were more types of languages in the universe than just human and angelic. He concluded that there is truly a divine language spoken audibly between the Godhead.

He also concluded that other types of languages are found in the gift of tongues. These other types of languages may never have been spoken by any race, class or kind of people but were and are created by God for the express purpose of being used in the gift of tongues.

Paul left the door of experience and the door of expectancy wide open. He saw no limit to the manner in which the Holy Spirit would speak through the believer, as long as what was spoken was truly a language.

Paul sees the gift of tongues as the lowest in rank among the spiritual gifts—apart from being accompanied by the gift of interpretation of tongues. Paul wanted the Corinthians to seek after all the spiritual gifts of the Holy Spirit, not just the gift of tongues.

In 1 Corinthians 12:29–31 Paul asks seven questions. The way these questions are written leaves room for nothing but negative answers. The negative particle μὴ (mē) is used seven times. This particle requires that the answer to all these questions be no.

What causes problems here is not so much the negative

particle μὴ (mē) as the Greek adjective πάς (päs). It does not have an article before it. For this reason this Greek adjective can only mean "a considerable portion."

What does this mean? It means that there were not many apostles, prophets, teachers, workers of miracles, those who had the gifts of healing, those who spoke in tongues and those who interpreted tongues.

While all these things were manifested in the early church, according to Paul, the majority of the saints at this time and even before did not hold these offices or did not experience these blessings. Why?

First, many new converts were fleeing paganism and had not received the baptism of the Holy Spirit, but had only been filled with the Holy Spirit at their conversion. (See Acts 8:15, 19; 9:17; 10:47; 19:2–6.) Therefore, due to this population explosion of believers, there were not very many exercising these blessings. There had not been enough time for all these converts to be taught that they needed to receive the baptism of the Holy Spirit in order to experience these blessings.

Second, the will of the believer must be calculated into this situation. Some believers may have been endowed with a certain office or gift but willed not to exercise it and had lost it. Further, the will of the Holy Spirit is a concern here. The Holy Spirit does not want every individual to be the same and have the same offices, abilities and capacities. (See 1 Corinthians 12:1–31.) The Holy Spirit is looking for those He can use in many different respects. He does not want believers to be clones.

Pertaining to the gifts of the Holy Spirit in these chapters, there are several reasons why few believers exercised these gifts:

- ✞ New converts had not yet received the baptism of the Holy Spirit.

- ✞ Some believers did not want the gifts at all or wanted gifts the Holy Spirit did not want them to have at that time.

✢ Some believers had lost the gifts of the Holy
Spirit that had been endowed upon them.

FIRST CORINTHIANS 13

In 1 Corinthians 13:1, Paul seems to say that the gift of
tongues includes tongues of men and of angels. This verse
has become highly controversial. The problem with 1
Corinthians 13:1 centers around the use of the subjunctive
mood by Paul.

What does Paul mean here by the subjunctive mood?
Some have concluded that he was stating a hypothetical
and theoretical case that never actually occurred during
his life. However, if this were true, then we must conclude
as well that Paul never spoke naturally in the tongues of
men. How ridiculous!

The subjunctive mood is found in what is known as the
more probable future conditional statement. This type of
conditional statement is used to indicate the prospect of
fulfillment in the future—with the expectation of it being
fulfilled—yet with some doubt or uncertainty that it will be.

Therefore the subjunctive mood and the more probable
future conditional statement used by Paul represent that:

✢ Paul expected himself to speak in tongues of
men and angels in the near future through the
gift of tongues.

✢ Paul saw the prospect of this fulfillment to be
most probable in the future.

✢ Paul recognized that the future manifestation of
the gift of tongues in his life and in what manner
that it appeared in the future was highly probable to be that of tongues of men and of angels.

✢ The experience of Paul with tongues shows that
he almost exclusively dealt with the tongues of
men and of angels.

✢ By using the subjunctive mood and the conditional statement, Paul set forth the view that in
the near future the gift of tongues in his life
would possibly not be the tongues of men and of

angels but tongues of some other type. He set forth the possibility that in his life he could, through the gift of tongues, speak in other languages that were not ones of men or angels. Paul sees all possibilities open here as long as what is spoken is a genuine language.

✞ By using the subjunctive mood, Paul recognizes that for the gift of tongues to be manifested, the will of the Holy Spirit and that of His vessels must agree. If a believer does not want the gifts of the Holy Spirit to be manifested in his life, the Holy Spirit will not force him to submit to them.

✞ On the other hand, if a believer wants a gift of the Holy Spirit to manifest itself at a particular time or occasion, the Holy Spirit may or may not so accommodate. There must be a meeting and agreement between the will of the Holy Spirit and the will of the believer for the gifts of the Holy Spirit to be manifested through that believer.

The fact that angels can have and speak their own languages is seen from the following arguments:

✞ First Corinthians 13:1 confirms that angels communicate with one another, whether audibly or inaudibly. (See Daniel 10:1–12:13; Zechariah 1:9–11; 2:3.)

✞ Such occurrences, found in verses about Abraham and Lot, illustrate angels' ability to speak audibly. (See Genesis 18–19.) Other instances, as in the case of Daniel, show angels' ability to speak inaudibly. (See Daniel 7–12.) Of course, in these instances the languages are human. Yet, they show that angels can speak audibly with spoken words or inaudibly with thoughts.

✞ Both the Old and New Testaments repeatedly recount that angels often appeared to humans and communicated with them. In these instances, the angels used human languages to communicate with humans. From this we can assume that angels know all human languages. They need not to learn them.

✞ On some occasions, angels use their own languages to communicate with others. In Job 1:6 and 2:1 the angels appeared along with Satan before the Lord God and communicated with one another and with the Lord. Satan spoke to God in an angelic language, not in a human language. Because Satan comes from the order of cherubim, Satan has his own language and dialect as well. However, the language he was using was not the cherubim language but the universal angelic language that all understand and know. Even the saints in heaven know this language.

✞ In Revelation 14:2–3, the 144,000 sang a new song that no man could learn, except the 144,000 Jews. This song was sung in an angelic language.

✞ The sound or voice out of heaven, mentioned in Revelation 14:2–3, was also not that of a human language but an angelic language.

✞ In 1 Kings 22:19–23, the hosts of heaven appeared before the Lord, and the Lord spoke in the universal angelic language to them and all other beings present. This universal angelic language was the universal language of creation. It was the only language Adam knew and the only language all humans knew before the tower of Babel. (See Genesis 10–11.) God spoke this language to Adam and Eve in the Garden of Eden. (See Genesis 3:9.) It was in this language that Adam gave the animals names. (See Genesis 2:20.) It was this language that the animals knew and the serpent spoke to deceive Eve. (See Genesis 3:1–24.)

✞ Notice that the wheel-angels have tongues with which they speak. They were saying unspeakable words that Ezekiel could not speak or comprehend. (See Ezekiel 3:13.) To a hearer of these angelic languages, unless God gives an interpretation, the languages are incomprehensible. This was what Paul meant by "unspeakable words" in 2 Corinthians 12:4.

✝ In 1 Enoch 14:9–23, written in the second century B.C., Enoch, having a vision of heaven, experienced the tongues of fire being part of the outer court of God's palace. The tongues of fire are angelic languages spoken in such a way that they are unspeakable words. In 1 Enoch 14:2, Enoch speaks of the tongue of flesh, that is, the languages of mankind. Therefore, Enoch contrasts the languages of mankind with the languages of angels. Tongues of fire in 1 Enoch are limited to angelic languages. Tongues as of fire in Acts 2 are not limited at all to just angelic languages; they are all-inclusive. In 1 Enoch 40 there is reference to the voices of the four archangels. Each voice magnifies God in different ways and in nonhuman languages.

✝ In 1 Corinthians 12:10–28, speaking with kinds of tongues is one of the gifts of the Holy Spirit. Paul thanks God that he spoke more in tongues than most men. (See 1 Corinthians 14:18.) In these kinds of languages are found the languages that angels possess, besides many other kinds that hardly can be imagined by men.

✝ Job 38:7 speaks of the sons of God, who are angels, shouting for joy over the work of creation. The point here is that the angels were speaking in another type of language that was not human, for this was before man was created.

✝ In the Testament of Job, reworked in the second century by Christians, the three daughters of Job spoke in the languages of angels and in angelic dialects. (See 48:3, 49:2; 50:2.) The Testament of Job speaks of at least four angelic dialects. It is believed that this book was rewritten before 1 Corinthians and that Paul used this work as a source for 1 Corinthians 13:1. This also shows that some humans, before the time of the gift of tongues, did speak with tongues of angels, though not because the gift of tongues had been bestowed upon them.

✝ In Revelation 4:5 it is said that voices came out of the throne of God. These voices were not human nor of human languages. These voices were at least angelic languages being spoken by angels or even the divine language spoken by the trinity.

✝ The ancient document 4 Maccabees, written in the first century, demonstrates the common belief (held especially in the Christian community) that angels have their own languages and within each order their own dialect. (See 4 Maccabees 10:21.)

✝ In the Ascension of Isaiah, written in the first century at the same time the apostles were living and the history recorded in Acts was being carried out, it is reported that the angels sang praises to God in their own tongue, not in a human tongue. This was truly an indication that within the early church, the gift of tongues was believed to incorporate the tongues of angels. (See Ascension of Isaiah 7:15–37.)

✝ In the Apocalypse of Abraham, an angel teaches Abraham the language of angels and an angelic hymn. The angelic hymn itself was taught to Abraham in the language of angels. However, it was also translated from that language to a human language. (See Apocalypse of Abraham 17.)

✝ While 1 Enoch, Testament of Job, 4 Maccabees, the Ascension of Isaiah and the Apocalypse of Abraham are not considered part of the Canon of Scriptures, they express here the common belief that angels can speak in human languages as well as their own. Moreover, since four of these works were either reworked or written by Christians in the first century, it reveals the opinion of the ancient church on the gift of tongues and on angelic languages. It states in one voice that angels have their own languages and their own dialects. It also states that the gift of tongues includes angelic languages. This view was so widespread that it found its place in these writings of the first century.

✟ It is Platoism and Philoism that teach that angels are formless and have no bodily form. This notion is not (and was not) found in ancient Judaism or the ancient church. (See Genesis 18:2–8, 19; Psalms 78:25; Exodus 24:9–11, Luke 22:30; Judges 6:11; 1 Corinthians 15:44; Daniel 10:5–7; 1 Chronicles 21:12–30).

OVERVIEW OF CHAPTER SIX

1 Corinthians 12

1. First Corinthians 12 lays out the organization of the gifts and their types.

2. First Corinthians 12 reveals to the church the position each person in the Godhead performs in relation to the gifts.

3. First Corinthians 12:7 teaches that the gifts are both for individual and collective profit.

4. First Corinthians 12:8–10 teaches that there are three classes of gifts:

   ✟ The first class is limited only to the gifts that refer to intellectual power.

   ✟ The second class is limited only to the gifts that refer to an exalted faith.

   ✟ The third class is limited only to the gifts that refer to tongues.

5. Though all gifts could be given to a person, Paul saw that it was more natural for the gifts to be given one at a time to the person.

6. To Paul, the gift of tongues is "kinds of tongues." This means that the gift of tongues is endowed

with families, classes, kinds, races, species and modes of tongues or languages.

7. In 1 Corinthians 12:29–31, it is understood that the majority of the saints at this time and even before did not hold these offices or did not experience these blessings. Why?

✠ Many new converts were rushing into the church from paganism.

✠ The will of a believer must be calculated into this situation.

✠ The new converts had not yet received the baptism of the Holy Spirit.

✠ Some believers did not want any of the gifts, or they wanted some gifts that the Holy Spirit, at that time, did not want them to have.

✠ Some believers had lost their endowment of the gifts of the Holy Spirit.

1 Corinthians 13

1. In 1 Corinthians 13:1 Paul sets forth, in difficult grammatical construction, the idea that the languages of men and of angels are not the only ones used with the gift of tongues but that the Holy Spirit can use tongues of every type and kind in this gift.

Chapter Seven

First Corinthians 14 on Tongues

Two thoughts must be kept in mind as we examine 1 Corinthians 14.

First, Paul is giving general statements about the characteristics and function of the gift of tongues. These statements are drawn from his own experiences, from what God Himself spoke to Paul about the gift of tongues and from the manifestations of this gift throughout other Christian communities. These statements represent the characteristics and function of this gift throughout all Christian communities.

Second, the restrictions cannot be seen as universal and perpetual but temporary, conditional and limited in effect only to the Corinthian church. This has been proved by the constant use of moods other than the indicative mood in Paul's text.

A MASS OF CONFLICTING THOUGHTS

First Corinthians 14, like Romans 7:15–21, is a mass of conflicting and contrasting thoughts. Paul weaves the characteristics and function of the gift of tongues amid the restrictions he placed on the gift of tongues for the Corinthian church only. In one instance, Paul asserts that the primary value of speaking in tongues is for the individual saint and as such edifies the person. (See 1 Corinthians 2:2–4; 14:28b.) In another place, however, he asserts that speaking in tongues should be used only for the edification of the church. (See 1 Corinthians 14:6–13, 23–25, 27–28a.)

Therefore, the thinking in 1 Corinthians 14, as it pertains to the gift of tongues, can only be that Paul is trying both to restrict the use of the gift of tongues in the Corinthian church and to free the gift of tongues for use in the rest of the Christian communities. As such, 1 Corinthians 14 expresses conflicting and opposing thoughts one after another about the gift of tongues.

Though it is true that there are sixteen contrasts between the gift of tongues and the gift of prophecy, it is also true that there are conflicting and opposing thoughts about the gift of tongues. In addition, Paul takes in 1 Corinthians 14 both a negative and positive view of the gift of tongues.

Modern critics of speaking in tongues lay too much emphasis on the negative and no emphasis on the positive. Further, the critics see the negative as embracing all Christians everywhere and the positive as embracing no Christians anywhere. Paul's negative view of speaking in tongues was limited, as I have already shown, to the Corinthian church alone. The positive view, however, is far-reaching and universal.

1 CORINTHIANS 14:2

In 1 Corinthians 14:2, Paul speaks of tongues in their praying capacity and states that when used in this manner they are not spoken to men but to God. This verse has been a windstorm of controversy. Those who deny the current existence of the gift of tongues have said that tongues in this verse are not of the Holy Spirit but of Satan.

One reason for this blasphemous conclusion is that the Greek noun θέος (thĕōs), which is translated *God*, does not have the article before it. For this reason, some have concluded that a pagan god is meant here. The problem with this interpretation is that the Greek noun θέος (thĕōs) in John 1:1c is also used without the article, and it refers to God the Word, not to a pagan god. Therefore there is inconsistency in the interpretation of 1 Corinthians 14:2 by those who deny the existence of the gift of tongues.

The Greek conjunction γάρ (gär) in 1 Corinthians 14:2 is used by Paul to give the reason for his preference of prophecy over the gift of tongues. It does not show that the gift of tongues he mentions in 1 Corinthians 14:2 is pagan, as some have imagined. In fact, this thought would be contrary to everything else Paul has said about the gift of tongues.

Using the Greek conjunction δέ (thĕ) in 1 Corinthians 14:3, Paul connects the gift of prophecy to the gift of tongues mentioned in 1 Corinthians 14:2 and states that they have originated from the same source. As a result, if the tongues mentioned are counterfeit, then the gift of prophecy mentioned by Paul must also be counterfeit. And if the gift of prophecy is counterfeit, then all that Paul speaks about must also be counterfeit. What nonsense! No Greek scholar worth his degree in Greek will support such ridiculous notions as these.

In 1 Corinthians 14, Paul gives sixteen contrasts between the gift of tongues and the gift of prophecy. Because the gift of prophecy is genuine, what it is contrasted with also must be genuine. For the contrast is between two gifts that are genuine, never counterfeit.

In addition, it is said by some that the singular form of the Greek noun γλῶσσα (glōsä) in 1 Corinthians 14:2, 4, 13–14, 19, 26 and 27 is used by Paul to define a difference between the counterfeit pagan phenomenon of speaking in tongues and the gift of tongues. In other words, when Paul uses the singular form of this Greek noun in these scriptures he is stressing that what is meant is not the genuine gift of tongues but rather the counterfeit. Problem! Paul, whether in the singular or plural, never in 1 Corinthians 14 uses this Greek noun to express the counterfeit. He always uses it to express the genuine.

The very use of the conjunction δέ (thĕ), as already shown, shows contrasts not between the genuine gift of tongues and a counterfeit, but between the gift of tongues with another gift of the Holy Spirit. In addition, this conjunction contrasts the function of tongues and the function of prophecy. (See 1 Corinthians 14:2–3.)

The Greek conjunction δέ (thĕ) noticeably contrasts speaking in tongues and prophecy in 1 Corinthians 14:3–4. This connects the singular use of the Greek noun γλῶσσα (glōsä) with the plural and states that the gift of tongues from the Holy Spirit is still being discussed. There is no counterfeit gift seen here. The very context of the Greek text and its very thought is destroyed if counterfeit gifts are introduced by Paul. Paul is dealing with the genuine gifts, not counterfeit gifts.

Turning back to 1 Corinthians 14:2, this verse emphasizes that the gift of tongues without interpretation—from all except God—is directed to God—not a pagan god but the true God. Additionally, it represents here the best way of communication now between God and man that can be used by man. Now all other ways of communication used by man can be hindered, blocked or even corrupted, but not the gift of tongues. It alone now is a direct line to God for man without any hindrance.

Also, the gift of tongues used in this fashion is covered in secrecy from all those who desire to understand what is being spoken. This is true even when a known language is used in this fashion. When a known language is used in this fashion God blinds all from understanding it, even if it is a common language.

Likewise, in 1 Corinthians 14:2–4, Paul states that the gift of tongues used for prayer is not meant for men to understand. The Greek verb ἀκούω (äkouō) used here denotes "to understand" rather than "to hear." This verb means "to hear" only in the sense of a mental appreciation of what is uttered, which is the same thing as "to understand." This verb is used in the same capacity in Acts 2:10–19.

According to Paul, the gift of tongues not for interpretation involves the spirit of man speaking secrets unconcealed. (See 1 Corinthians 14:2, 14.) It is the Holy Spirit speaking through the spirit of man by means of his tongue that secrets are unconcealed.

That the spirit spoken of in 1 Corinthians 14:2 is the spirit of man is seen from the following arguments:

✝ First Corinthians 12–14 is written by Paul as a separate subject and a separate segment from all other parts of 1 Corinthians.

✝ In 1 Corinthians 12, Paul speaks about the Holy Spirit several times and every time he uses the article. In 1 Corinthians 14, the Greek noun πνεῦμα (pnĕvmä) does not have the article.

✝ Every time the Holy Spirit is mentioned in the Greek as πνεύματι (pnĕvmäti), the article is present. In 1 Corinthians 14 the article is absent.

✝ In 1 Corinthians 14:32 the Greek noun πνεῦμα (pnĕvmä) is used without the article and denotes the spirit of man. This is an indication that Paul is stressing in 1 Corinthians 14:2 only the spirit of man.

✝ Every time in 1 Corinthians where the Holy Spirit is spoken of in the Greek as πνεύματι (pnĕvmäti), the definite article accompanies it.

✝ In 1 Corinthians 14:2 there is a comparison between understanding and the spirit, like that found in 1 Corinthians 14:14–16. The "one" who does not understand is the same as the "one who speaks mysteries."

✝ Paul is not stressing the part that the Holy Spirit plays in the gift of tongues, but the part that man plays.

The Greek noun πνεῦμα (pnĕvmä), used here, does not denote the entire inner man. If that were the case, then understanding would be seen as part of it. On the contrary, the Greek noun πνεῦμα (pnĕvmä) denotes here the power and capacity of the inner man when it yields itself to the direction, supervision, influence and power of the Holy Spirit. The understanding of man comes from the Greek noun νοῦς (nous) and denotes here the power and capacity of the inner man apart from the Holy Spirit when it acts separately from the Holy Spirit.

In other words, it means a state of passive receptivity by which the exercise of free will and self-consciousness is yielded to the divine influence of the Holy Spirit, and the Holy Spirit uses the tongue of the individual as His mouthpiece.

The Greek noun voῦς (nous) means the thinking power of the mind as it pertains to words and thoughts. This thinking power of the mind is bypassed when the gift of tongues is operated by the Holy Spirit. The words come not from the intellectual framework of man but from the intelligence and vocabulary of the Holy Spirit. By this the Holy Spirit is able to express Himself in the human sphere of direct feeling and intuition without any hindrance from the mind of an individual, who can hinder what the Spirit desires to speak.

In 1 Corinthians 14:15, Paul contrasts the spirit with the understanding. He contrasts praying in the spirit with praying in understanding, singing in the spirit with singing in understanding, blessing in the spirit with blessing in understanding, and giving thanks in the spirit with giving thanks in understanding. He shows that the understanding plays no part in speaking in tongues, whether praying tongues or ministering tongues.

However, the understanding is involved in the interpretation of ministering tongues. The words "spirit" and "understanding" denote the same thing here as they do in 1 Corinthians 14:2.

1 Corinthians 14:4

First Corinthians 14:4 has been argued by some actually to be Paul rebuking the practice of speaking in tongues for the sake of edifying oneself. According to this argument, there is no such thing as speaking in tongues for personal edification. This, however, is nonsense! There is no hint of this in the Greek text.

This hardly fits the context thought by Paul when he goes on to encourage speaking in tongues. (See 1 Corinthians 14:5.) The view that supports tongues being used for self-edification is necessary because of what is said in verse 5—that if a person can interpret, he can edify not only himself, but also the church.

Furthermore, Paul contrasts—by using the Greek conjunction δέ (thĕ)—both the gift of tongues used without interpretation except from God and the gift of prophecy. If Paul is rebuking the Corinthians for using the gift of tongues to edify themselves, then he is also rebuking the same Corinthians for using the gift of prophecy to edify the church.

Neither can 1 Corinthians 10:23–24 be used to prove that 1 Corinthians 14:4 is truly a rebuke. In 1 Corinthians 10:23–24, Paul is not prohibiting the Christian from using his liberty for his own profit or edification, but prohibiting the Christian from using his liberty at the expense of someone else—a fact that is asserted in the context of chapters 8–10.

In addition, the point by Paul in 1 Corinthians 14:22–24 is that praying tongues edify the person speaking them and are more for the benefit of the individual Christian than the entire congregation. Yet, as we will see, even praying tongues can be a benefit for the congregation.

Praying tongues are a private affair for self-edification. (See 1 Corinthians 14:2–4.) They are a devotional practice for the purpose of communicating with God as the Holy Spirit gives the utterance. The Holy Spirit, through the gift of tongues, may indeed be praying for the individual to God the Father, God the Son and also to Himself. Any or all of the three divine Persons may be the One (or Ones) who are being prayed to through the gift of tongues. The devotional practice must not diminish the preaching of the gospel but bear testimony of it.

Praying tongues uttered in public were condemned by Paul at Corinth. Nonetheless, this restriction was limited to the Corinthian church because of their carnality and immaturity. No such restriction was or is given for the other Christian communities.

A church may set aside time for this devotional practice before services, after services or even during services and accompany it with songs of praise and adoration for a sign to unbelievers and believers alike. (See Isaiah 28:11–12.) The devotional practice, when exercised in a service, will accompany the moving of the Holy Spirit, bear witness to Him, bear witness to the message of the gospel and bear witness to the Word of God.

Therefore, praying tongues, when used in this fashion, are seen as a benefit for the entire congregation, for a church meeting, for an individual church and even for all Christian communities. The reasons for this are as follows:

- ✟ Praying tongues are a vivid and visible sign of the presence of the Holy Spirit, His confirmation of the message of the gospel and His confirmation of the Word of God.

- ✟ They become a beacon of the cross, of the apostolic faith, of the Christian's first love, of the unadulterated message of the gospel with power. In this way they become very beneficial to the whole congregation even though the messages given are not to be interpreted by the gift of interpretation of tongues or are found within a particular church to be incomprehensible.

- ✟ The utterances are like water in the midst of a desert. They refresh the whole congregation with the assurance that the Holy Spirit is present, that the message of the gospel is confirmed as true and that the Word of God is confirmed as true.

- ✟ Praying tongues are given in the form of prayers.

- ✟ It is the Holy Spirit who utters the prayers.

- ✟ He does so for the person He is using to speak to other individuals, for the entire Christian community and to a particular church. It is unethical to state that praying tongues provide no benefit to the entire Christian community or a particular church.

✞ Praying tongues are a means by which the Holy Spirit can pray for a particular church.

✞ They are a means by which the Holy Spirit can express His concerns, wants and desires to the other members of the Godhead about a particular church.

✞ They are a means by which the Holy Spirit can grieve over a certain situation in a congregation.

✞ They are also a means by which the Holy Spirit can intercede for a particular church. If there is no benefit to a particular church in being prayed for by the Holy Spirit, then the Holy Spirit has lost His place in that church.

Because tongues, whether praying tongues or ministering tongues, are the very utterances of the Holy Spirit through a human vehicle, they are then the words of the Holy Spirit Himself. How can the utterance of the Holy Spirit be wrong? It cannot be!

While Paul recognized this, he placed restrictions on the utterance of the Holy Spirit in the midst of a service as a direct result of the carnality and immaturity of the Corinthians. Even Paul in the midst of all these restrictions admits in verse 28b that praying tongues can be spoken in the midst of a service. He says, "But let him speak to himself and to God."

Paul allows for praying tongues to be used in a church meeting, but not if it causes disorder or confusion or draws attention away from the Word of God. The idea of the speaker speaking to himself is the same as the speaker edifying himself.

The personal edification must be defined. In 1 Corinthians 14:4, the Greek verb οἰκοδομέω (ēkōthōmĕō) denotes something that promotes growth and development in Christian wisdom, affection, grace, virtue, holiness and blessedness. Paul sees praying tongues as a great benefit to the Christian walk. He believes that praying tongues help promote the building up, strengthening and establishing of the spiritual growth and development of an individual Christian in association with the Word of God.

Praying tongues, like all other gifts or their functions, can only work, operate and do what the believer permits and allows. (See 1 Corinthians 14:32.) So, the praying tongue can only promote as the believer allows, and this process at Corinth was only partial. This leads to the fact that many of the Corinthians, even with praying tongues, were carnal, immature and even confused. One must always recognize:

> ☩ The exercise of free will in such situations as this when these gifts are being used through men.

> ☩ The carnality and confusion among the Corinthians were not a result of the spiritual gifts in any way, but a result of the fact that the Corinthians themselves had not reached maturity and had not fully understood the operation of such gifts. (See 1 Corinthians 14:20.)

> ☩ The Corinthians were baptized babes; they had not yet had enough time to study and become knowledgeable in the ways of God and His Spirit. Yet, God operated through these babes.

> ☩ The misuse of the gifts rests on the fact that the Corinthians were still babes. Though the saints were edified through praying tongues, this edification was in many respects partial for many persons.

> ☩ Even with the gifts being manifested in the Corinthian church, many were still carnal and immature. Paul exhorts them to stop being infants and reach maturity.

1 CORINTHIANS 14:5

If Paul hated the gift of tongues, why does he in 1 Corinthians 14:5 state such a strong wish about it? This must be seen as a powerful desire of Paul's and not an unworthy concession to the Corinthians over their partiality for this gift. This is evident from the fact that he goes on at once to address prophecy as the higher and worthier gift, which he still more earnestly desires that they should have and exercise.

There is no way that the Greek adjective πᾶς (păs) can mean "all" in this use. On the contrary, Paul saw only a minority of people speaking in tongues in the Corinthian church. He did not see all Corinthians speaking in tongues. He was at best hopeful that many would, though it is indicated that he believed that was too much to hope for.

The words "except he may interpret" need to be examined. Understanding this expression from the Greek destroys any conclusion about the gift of tongues being meant for only one function. The gift of tongues by this expression alone is seen to split off into two main divisions.

The first division and the only one mentioned for the first four verses is praying tongues, which are never to be interpreted by men. The second division is ministering tongues. It is ridiculous to take the Greek verb διερμηνεύω (theĕrmēnĕvō) as firm proof that the tongues spoken are only tongues of men. It is true that the Greek verb διερμηνεύω (theĕrmēnĕvō) can be translated "translate" easily. (See Luke 24:27; Acts 9:36; 1 Corinthians 12:30; 14:5, 13, 27.) However, any genuine language can be translated and interpreted. Both translation and interpretation work together. No Greek scholar supports that this Greek verb can be used as proof that the tongues are only those of men.

Further, this Greek verb is found in the subjunctive mood. The subjunctive mood is important. Paul stresses that tongues used for interpretation by men are used mainly for edification of the church. However, by using the subjunctive mood, Paul sees that ministering tongues may be used not only for the edification of the church, but also for the edification of the speaker himself or someone else.

He sees that ministering tongues are primarily used to edify a particular church or the whole church community. In addition to this, there is a possibility that ministering tongues, under the guidance of the Holy Spirit, can be used to edify the speaker or even an individual other than the speaker.

Paul discusses his experience with ministering tongues and reports that he mostly saw them being used to edify a particular church or the whole church community, while on some occasions he saw the speaker or another individual being edified. Paul sees no limit to how the ministering tongues can be used in reference to interpretation. Paul also expects to experience tongues with the gift of interpretation in the near future.

1 CORINTHIANS 14:6–12

First Corinthians 14:6–12 is the first restriction of 1 Corinthians 14. Paul's purpose here is not only to retrain the Corinthian body in their use of the gift of tongues, but also to retrain them in their use of ministering tongues. For this purpose, Paul compares praying tongues and ministering tongues.

Paul compares praying tongues to an "uncertain" sound. Therefore, speaking in tongues was useless for the Corinthian church (due to their carnality and immaturity), unless it was heard and distinctly understood by means of the interpretation of tongues.

Paul states that it is better for the Corinthian church that he and any other minister not come to them speaking in tongues, but speaking in revelation, knowledge, prophecy or doctrine through the word of wisdom, the word of knowledge and the gift of prophecy. Apparently Paul believed that all those who would come ministering to the Corinthian church should not speak to them in tongues lest they make the situation in the church worse.

First Corinthians 14:6–12 is written proof that Paul already had warned all the other Christian communities not to come to Corinth speaking in tongues, but to refrain from it because of the Corinthians' carnality and immaturity.

Paul, in 1 Corinthians 14:12, states that for the Corinthians it is better that they excel in those things that have a chance of edifying their particular church. Paul writes: "So also you, since you are zealots of spiritual things, seek [or strive] for the edification of the church in order that you may excel." Here Paul describes the Corinthians as zealots of spiritual things.

From 1 Corinthians 14:12, several things are understood from the Greek grammar:

✞ The Corinthians were stirred to action by strong emotions about spiritual things.

✞ They were zealous about spiritual things; they ardently desired to join, promote, actively support, possess and defend spiritual things, especially the spiritual gifts.

✞ This zealousness indicates that they, being carnal and immature, did not place any restraint on spiritual things.

✞ The restraint came not from Paul's restrictions, but from testing the spirit of truth from the spirit of error through the Word of God. (See 1 John 5:5–10.)

✞ Paul concluded that it was far better for them to seek those gifts that edified their church than the ones that edified the individual Christian.

✞ Paul did not refute the use of spiritual gifts that would not edify the church. He was simply restraining the Corinthian saints in their use of spiritual gifts because of their carnality and immaturity.

✞ Paul stated to the Corinthian church that seeking spiritual things would result in the edification of the church and that for this reason they all should seek spiritual things. For the sake of the Corinthians, and only for their concern, Paul tells them that personal edification is primarily a byproduct of seeking spiritual things.

✞ Paul asserted, for the sake of the Corinthians, that the edification of the church was more important than the edification of the individual.

✞ It is seen that the Corinthians had taught the extreme opposite.

✞ Paul took the extreme approach and went in the opposite direction.

✞ Paul hoped that the Corinthians would arrive at the point that they could see the gifts of the Holy Spirit could be used to edify the church as well as the individual Christian. (See 1 Corinthians 14:2-4.)

✞ Paul strongly asserted that for the Corinthians, because of their carnality and immaturity, the object of their edification needed to be their particular church.

✞ Paul pushed them very strongly. He exhorted them to seek spiritual things—in particular, spiritual gifts—that would edify the church.

✞ Paul doubted that the Corinthians could be pushed in the opposite direction. This is seen by his use of the *imperative mood*.

✞ Undoubtedly, Paul believed that the carnality and immaturity of the Corinthians would continue and that they would continue to exalt all spiritual things that edified the individual instead of their church. He thought they were a lost cause; nevertheless, he exhorted them to change.

1 CORINTHIANS 14:13–14

In 1 Corinthians 14:13–14, Paul exhorted those who spoke in ministering tongues to pray that they could interpret as well. The Corinthians were speaking praying tongues publicly, which Paul condemned in only the Corinthian church.

Paul in 1 Corinthians 14:14 says why he exhorted any person who spoke in tongues at Corinth to pray for interpretation. Remember, all of this was his argument for the

Corinthians to abandon all gifts or functions of gifts that edify only the individual. He was pushing them to move in the extreme opposite direction in hopes that they would end up in the middle of the road. According to Greek grammar, Paul meant that:

✝ He himself expected to speak in tongues in the near future through the gift of tongues.

✝ He saw the prospect of this fulfillment to be most probable in the future.

✝ He recognized that the future manifestation of the gift of tongues in his own life would be manifested by his spirit praying while his understanding would be useless, meaningless and without fruit.

✝ He saw his spirit active in the gift of tongues, not his understanding.

✝ He saw that the understanding could be active if the gift of interpretation of tongues is found and used. The understanding is active only through the Holy Spirit giving the interpretation to one's understanding.

✝ He stated that the understanding is at all times useless and without fruit in this phenomenon, but not in the interpretation of tongues.

✝ The reason is, the understanding is unfruitful and useless when praying tongues are spoken; the understanding is active when ministering tongues are used with interpretation.

1 CORINTHIANS 14:18

According to Greek grammar, Paul does not give thanks to God that he speaks in tongues more than anyone else. He does thank God that he speaks in tongues more than most saints of that time. This is a clear indication that Paul did not proclaim that he more than any other spoke in tongues, only that he spoke in tongues more than most who spoke in tongues in the Corinthian church. Paul may be thinking of some brother or sister who he believed spoke in tongues even more than he did.

Paul uses the singular, *tongue*, in the text. He does this to indicate that he speaks in his particular tongue more than most who speak in their own divinely-given tongue, whether it is the same, similar or even different. According to this, Paul was endowed only with one language and not many.

1 CORINTHIANS 14:19

In this verse, Paul contrasts what he said in verse 18 with what he said in verse 19. He prefers to speak five words with his understanding in a public meeting than to speak ten thousand words in tongues without an interpretation. He sets forth a reason for the restriction at Corinth against praying tongues being used publicly. However this is only for the Corinthians who were immature and carnal.

1 CORINTHIANS 14:23

Paul in 1 Corinthians 14:23 again uses the subjunctive mood and the conditional statement that accompanies it. From this conditional statement one can easily conclude that:

- ✝ Paul expected the Corinthians to come together in a church meeting in the near future.
- ✝ Paul expected many would continue to simultaneously speak in tongues in that church meeting.
- ✝ Paul also expected the unlearned and unbelievers to enter the service.
- ✝ He probably also believed that those who were either unlearned or unbelievers would conclude that the Corinthians had gone mad.
- ✝ Paul, however, indicates that there is a possibility that the Corinthians would not meet again in the near future and that none would speak in tongues.
- ✝ Paul also sees the possibility that, even with the practice of speaking in tongues in a church

meeting, the unlearned or unbelievers may not see the believers as madmen.

Paul saw here that not all members of the Corinthian church were present in every meeting. This is known because of the Greek adjective for "all" not having the article before it. This is in accordance with 1 Corinthians 14:5, in which Paul sees only a minority of people speaking in tongues in the Corinthian church.

1 CORINTHIANS 14:24–26

Paul, by using the subjunctive mood in 1 Corinthians 14:26, set forth verse 26 as part of 1 Corinthians 14:23–25. All these verses compose one large *more probable conditional statement* that has two parts. One part deals with tongues; the other deals with prophecy.

In verse 25 Paul sees another plausible scenario for the Corinthian church that he expects to occur in the near future. He expects that, if the Corinthians heed his advice, in the near future many Corinthian saints will prophesy one by one in the public meeting and those who are unlearned or unbelievers will be convicted and judged by all that is said.

On the other hand, Paul also expects that if the Corinthians will not heed his advice, then praying tongues will continue to be spoken publicly by the Corinthians. Paul condemned this at Corinth due to their carnality and immaturity.

1 CORINTHIANS 14: 27–28A

The phrase "if anyone speaks in a tongue" is seen from the Greek as a simple condition. What does this mean? By Paul using this type of conditional sentence he does not denounce speaking in tongues at all. He sets forth the view that speaking in tongues is certainly a part of the Christian experience. Further, he recognizes that the Holy Spirit calls all to experience this whether they accept this call or not.

The last part of this conditional statement reads, "Let it

be by two or at the most three, and in succession, and let someone interpret." This part is an exhortation and plea (in the imperative mood) by Paul to the Corinthians that the use of the gift of tongues in a church meeting will follow this succession.

Here Paul speaks not of praying tongues but of ministering tongues. He pleads that the ministering tongues spoken in the Corinthian church be by two or three for the sole purpose of interpretation. Paul does not exclude the speaker as the one who has the ability to interpret his own message. (See 1 Corinthians 14:13.) This restriction, like all others, is limited only to the Corinthian church.

1 CORINTHIANS 14: 34–35

Because 1 Corinthians 14 deals in particular with the restrictions of spiritual gifts placed solely on the Corinthian church, then the restriction against women speaking in church, mentioned in 1 Corinthians 14:34–35, is limited only to the Corinthian church. This restriction was not placed on the Corinthian women in general, but only when they prophesied and spoke in tongues together or all at the same time in the Corinthian church. So, the restriction never demanded that women in all other Christian communities keep silent! Only at Corinth and only when several spoke all together in prophecy and in tongues.

It is not Paul's desire to condemn women to absolute silence in the church. If this were the case, then no word at all could be uttered by a woman in church.

From verses 14:6–39, the word for "speak" is the Greek verb λαλέω (lälĕō), and on every occasion found in 1 Corinthians 14 it refers to nothing but spiritual gifts and their regulations in the Corinthian church.

In verse 34, the Greek verb λαλέω (lälĕō) is used to express the immaturity within the Corinthian church in using the spiritual gifts, especially prophecy and tongues for interpretation. Some will most likely point to the plurality of "church" in 1 Corinthians 14:34 as firm proof that this restriction must be universal, affecting all Christian communities. However, it is contrary to the whole thought process that all church communities are meant here.

Turning to Greek evidence, there is a difference in the manuscripts. One group of manuscripts uses the plural for church. The other uses the singular for church. According to the Patristic evidence, the early church read their text in the singular.[1]

Even if the plural number is kept, the thought is limited to the Corinthian church. Paul can and does speak of one church in a particular place in plural terms and does often speak of the universal church of God as "churches." (See Galatians 1:2; 1 Corinthians 16:1.) The point is that the church in focus here is the Corinthian church, not any other Christian community.

The singular stresses the Corinthian Christian community as a whole. The plural stresses all the groups, divisions and factions of the Corinthian church.

1 CORINTHIANS 14:39

In 1 Corinthians 14:39 Paul tells the Corinthians not to forbid the function of ministering tongues within the church service. Some still wanted speaking in tongues to be present in the church service while another faction hated all speaking in tongues. This is clear from Paul's use of the imperative mood in the present tense to form a prohibition. A prohibition used in the present tense indicates a desire for a person or persons to obey and stop doing what is already in process.

OVERVIEW OF CHAPTER SEVEN

When studying 1 Corinthians 14, two thoughts must be kept in mind:

- ✝ First, Paul is giving general statements about the characteristics and function of the gift of tongues.
- ✝ Second, his restrictions are not universal.

A Mass of Conflicting Thoughts

1. First Corinthians 14 is seen as a mass of conflicting and contrasting thoughts.

2. It is true that there are sixteen contrasts made between the gift of tongues and the gift of prophecy.

3. There are also conflicting and opposing thoughts about the gift of tongues.

4. Paul takes both a negative and a positive view about the gift of tongues.

1 Corinthians 14:2

1. Paul speaks of praying in tongues as a form of prayer.

2. God, when Paul speaks of Him in this verse, is not a pagan god but the true Lord and God.

3. This verse gives one reason for Paul's preference of prophecy over the gift of tongues.

4. The Greek connects both tongues mentioned in 1 Corinthians 14:2 with that of divine prophecy, which means that both are genuine.

5. The gift of tongues mentioned in this verse cannot be counterfeit.

6. The singular use of *tongue* cannot be used to prove the genuine tongues from the counterfeit tongues.

7. This verse emphasizes that the gift of tongues without interpretation is directed to God.

8. From this one verse, it is understood that all other ways of communication now used by man can be hindered, blocked or even corrupted, but not the gift of tongues.

9. For the gift of tongues without interpretation,

the spirit of man speaks secrets unconcealed.
(See 1 Corinthians 14:2, 14.)

10. The noun *spirit* is understood to be the spirit of
man rather than the Holy Spirit.

11. The noun *spirit* does not mean the entire inner
man.

1 Corinthians 14:4

1. Paul is not rebuking the practice of speaking in
tongues. (See 1 Corinthians 14.)

2. Paul recognizes the difference between praying
tongues and ministering tongues.

3. To Paul, praying in tongues is a private affair for
self-edification. (See 1 Corinthians 14:2–4.)

4. Praying tongues were condemned by Paul at the
Corinthian church because of the church's carnality and immaturity.

5. No such restriction was applied to the other
Christian communities.

6. The benefits of praying tongues include:

  ✝ A vivid and visible sign of the presence of the Holy
  Spirit, His confirmation of the message of the
  gospel and His confirmation of the Word of God.

  ✝ A beacon of the cross, of the apostolic faith, of
  the first love of the Christian, of the unadulterated message of the gospel with power.

  ✝ A blessing to the whole congregation.

  ✝ Utterances that refresh the entire congregation
  with the assurance that the Holy Spirit is
  present.

  ✝ A form of prayer.

  ✝ The Holy Spirit is uttering prayers.

  ✝ A means by which the Holy Spirit can pray for a
  particular church.

  ✝ A means by which the Holy Spirit can express His

concerns, wants and desires to the other members of the Godhead about a particular church.

✟ A means by which the Holy Spirit can grieve over a certain situation within a congregation.

✟ A means by which the Holy Spirit can enter into intercession for a particular church.

7. The Holy Spirit is the one who is speaking, whether through praying tongues or ministering tongues.

8. Personal edification promotes growth and development in Christian wisdom, affection, grace, virtue, holiness and blessedness.

9. Praying tongues, like all other gifts or their functions, can only work, operate and do what the believer allows. (See 1 Corinthians 14:32.)

1 Corinthians 14:5

1. First Corinthians 14:5 proves that Paul does not hate the gift of tongues.

2. This verse proves that the gift of tongues does not express one function, but two.

1 Corinthians 14:6–12

1. This is the first restriction on the gift of tongues.

2. From 1 Corinthians 14:12, several things are understood from the Greek grammar:

✟ The Corinthians were stirred to action by strong emotions about spiritual things.

✟ They were zealous or eager about spiritual things.

✟ This zealousness indicates that they, being carnal and immature, did not put any restraint on spiritual things.

✟ The restraint came not from Paul's restrictions, but from testing the spirit of truth from the spirit of error through the Word of God. (See 1 John 5:5-1.).

✝ Paul concluded that it was far better for them to seek those gifts that would edify the church than those that would edify the individual Christian.

✝ Paul did not refute the use of spiritual gifts that do not edify the church; he simply restrained this use in the lives of the Corinthian saints because of their carnality and immaturity.

✝ Paul stated to the Corinthian church that seeking spiritual things would result in the edification of the church, and it was this goal that they all should seek.

✝ Paul asserted, for the sake of the Corinthians, that the edification of the church was more important than the edification of the individual.

✝ It is seen that the Corinthians had taught the extreme opposite.

✝ Paul took the extreme approach and went in the opposite direction.

✝ Paul hoped that the Corinthians would arrive at more of a middle ground in their practice.

1 Corinthians 14:13–14

In 1 Corinthians 14:13–14, Paul gives the reason he exhorts any person who speaks in tongues at Corinth to pray for interpretation.

1 Corinthians 14:18

According to Greek grammar, Paul did not speak in tongues more than anyone else. He did speak in tongues more than many.

1 Corinthians 14:19

In this verse, Paul states that he prefers to speak five words with his understanding in a public meeting than to speak ten thousand words in tongues without interpretation of those tongues.

1 Corinthians 14:23

Paul says that the unlearned or unbelievers may think the believers to be mad if they spoke in tongues.

1 Corinthians 14:24–26

Paul hopes that the Corinthians will use the gift of prophecy more than the gift of tongues.

1 Corinthians 14: 27–28a

The phrase "if anyone speaks in a tongue" is seen from the Greek as a simple condition. By using this, Paul sets forth the view that speaking in tongues is certainly a part of the Christian experience.

1 Corinthians 14: 34–35

The restriction against women mentioned in these verses is limited only to the Corinthian church.

1 Corinthians 14:39

Paul tells the Corinthians not to forbid ministering tongues within the church service.

Chapter Eight

Purposes for
the Gift of Tongues

This chapter comprises a quick reference of twenty-four biblically stated purposes for the gift of tongues.

1. The gift of tongues is seen as a sign of the Holy Spirit's presence. (See Mark 16:17; 1 Corinthians 14:22; Acts 10:44–46; 11:16–17; 15:7–9.)

2. The gift of tongues is also seen not as a qualification for the fullness of the Holy Spirit but as an indication of that fullness. (See Mark 16:17; 1 Corinthians 14:22; Acts 10:44–46; 11:16–17; 15:7–9.)

3. The gift of tongues is for self-edification. (See 1 Corinthians 14:4.)

4. The gift of tongues is for the edification of the church as a whole. (See 1 Corinthians 14:5.)

5. The gift of tongues is for communication with God for personal edification. (See 1 Corinthians 14:5.)

6. The gift of tongues is ordained by God for the church. (See 1 Corinthians 12:28; 14:21.)

7. The gift of tongues is the initial evidence—not all evidence—of the baptism of the Holy Spirit. (See John 15:26; Acts 2:4; 10:45–46; 19:6; 15:8.)

8. The apostle Paul was thankful to God that he spoke in tongues. (See 1 Corinthians 14:18.)

9. The apostle Paul wanted saints to speak in tongues. (See 1 Corinthians 14:5.)

10. The gift of tongues is one of the gifts of the Spirit. (See 1 Corinthians 12:8–10.)

11. The gift of tongues is a fulfillment of prophecy. (See Isaiah 28:11–12; 1 Corinthians 14:21; Joel 2:28.)

12. The gift of tongues is proof of the resurrection and the exaltation of Jesus Christ. (See John 16:7; Acts 2:22, 25, 32–33.)

13. The gift of tongues is the means by which the Holy Spirit is able to intercede for a saint through prayer. (See Romans 8:26; 1 Corinthians 14:14.)

14. The gift of tongues is for singing in the Spirit, praying in the Spirit, and even speaking in the Spirit. (See 1 Corinthians 14:1–36.)

15. Paul demands that speaking in tongues should not be forbidden. (See 1 Corinthians 14:39.)

16. Speaking in tongues confirms the Word of God. (See Mark 16:17, 20.)

17. The gift of tongues may be a sign that one is a believer. (See Mark 16:17; John 7:38–39.)

18. The gift of tongues is a sign to the unbeliever positively for conviction or negatively for judgment. (See 1 Corinthians 14:22; Isaiah 28:11–12.)

19. Speaking in tongues is spoken of by Isaiah as a "rest." (See Isaiah 28:11–12.)

20. Speaking in tongues is spoken of by Isaiah as a "refreshing." (See Isaiah 28:11–12.)

21. The gift of tongues is a special gift that is identified with the church and even all other New Testament saints. (See 1 Corinthians 14:28; 21.)

22. The gift of tongues is given so men can speak supernaturally to God. (See 1 Corinthians 14:2.)

23. The gift of tongues is given so men can magnify God. (See Acts 10:46.)

24. The gift of tongues is given so the spirits of men can pray. (See 1 Corinthians 14:14.)

Notes

INTRODUCTION
1. *Ignatius to the Tarsians*, 2.

CHAPTER ONE
THE TERM TONGUES AND ITS USE: PART I
1. Clement of Alexandria, *Stromata*, 1:21.
2. Tertullian, *Tertullian against Marcion*, 5:8.
3. *Constitutions of the Holy Apostles*, 8:1.

CHAPTER THREE
THE EVENT OF ACTS 2:2–4
1. Irenæus, *Irenæus against Heresies*, 3:17:2, 5:6:1.
2. *Didache*, 11.
3. Piepenbring, C. H., *Theology of the Old Testament*, 86–88.
4. *Origen Against Celsus*, 7:8–10.
5. Ibid, 7:9.
6. *Irenæus Against Heresies*, 1:13:3.
7. *Origen Against Celsus*, 7:7.
8. *Fragments of Papais*, 1–10.
9. *Irenæus against Heresies*, 3:17:2.
10. Tertullian, *On Fasting, in Opposition to the Psychics*, 10.

CHAPTER FOUR
THE BAPTISM OF THE HOLY SPIRIT
1. The Greek constructions for the baptism into Christ are εἰς Χριστὸν ἐβαπτίσθητε in Galatians 3:27 and ἐβαπτίσθημεν εἰς Χριστὸν Ἰησοῦν in Romans 6:3. On the other hand, the Greek constructions for the baptism of the Holy Spirit are βαπτίσει ἐν πνεύματι ἁγίῳ καὶ πυρί in Matthew 3:11, βαπτίσει ἐν πνεύματι ἁγίῳ in Mark 1:8, βαπτίσει ἐν πνεύματι ἁγίῳ καὶ πυρί in Luke 3:16, ὁ βαπτίζων ἐν πνεύματι ἁγίῳ in John 1:33, ἐν πνεύματι βαπτισθήσεσθε ἁγίῳ in Acts 1:5, βαπτισθήσεσθε ἐν πνεύατι ἁγίῳ in Acts 11:16, τὴν δωρεὰν τοῦ ἁγίου πνεύματος in Acts 2:28, and ἡ δωρεὰ τοῦ ἁγίου πνεύματος in Acts 10:45.
2. Tertullian, *Exhortation to Chastity*, 4.
3. Cyprian, *The Epistles of Cyprian*, 74:10.
4. Anonymous bishop, *A Treatise on Re-Baptism*, 17.
5. Ibid., 1–16.

Chapter Five
1 Corinthians on Tongues

1. *The First Epistle of Clement to the Corinthians*, 19, 23, 32.
2. *The Epistle of Ignatius to the Philippians*, 2.
3. Irenæus, *Irenæus Against Heresies*, 5:6:1.
4. *Didache*, 11.
5. Novatian, *A Treatise Concerning the Trinity*, 29.
6. Irenæus, *Irenæus Against Heresies*, 5:6:1; Tertullian Against Marcion, 4:8.

Chapter Seven
1 Corinthians 12–13 on Tongues

1. *The Treatises of Cyprian*, p. 46.

For more information about Dr. Roberts, his mother, their schedule of events, their ministry or donations to their ministry, write to:

True Light Ministries
P.O. Box 28538
Jacksonville, FL 32218
A Non-Profit and Tax-Exempt Organization
Cell: 904-472-7786 • Fax: 904-751-0304
truelightministries.org

For I shall bring forth truth out of darkness for the sake of my people.